Firstly, a big thank you to all my readers for reaching out for this Business Plan book.

It was January 2020 when I realised, I could not order any container loads of my products. All the factories were closed, and people were only allowed out of their homes to go for provisions. I looked for where I could go and help protect vulnerable people from the nasty bug. I instructed my accountants to suspend my business and within a month I was a Keyworker Care Assistant with the Nurses on accelerated training. Whilst helping to prepare for the worst I wrote this book. It is the book that I wanted to read when I started up my first business so I know you will enjoy the journey of this 'The Business Mountain' book.

The first in a 10-volume series where I share all I have learned on my journey to help with yours!

Thx

Virginia

Publisher
The Business Mountain Publishing

Copyright © Virginia Rabbitts, 2022

First paperback edition 2023
Version 002

ISBN (Paperback) 978-1-3999-2263-0
ISBN (Hardback) 978-1-7393-8040-3

Text design and layout by Virginia Rabbits.

Brand and design by
Victoria How Design (victoriahow.co.uk).

This book was typeset in Literata with
DM Serif and Outfit as display typefaces.

THE BUSINESS
Mountain

10-Volume Business Book Series

BY VIRGINIA RABBITTS

"Business Plan is incredibly comprehensive."

THE BUSINESS
Mountain

BOOK 2

Business Plan

BY VIRGINIA RABBITTS

Foreword

Preparing a great business plan takes a great deal of time, thought and contemplation. It's worth noting that it's completely possible to run a business without having any form of a written business plan at all. Many people do all over the world do so and that's fine.

If you want to raise capital for your business, or choose to work with other businesses, you may decide that you need to create your own business and marketing plans for your own peace of mind.

Both business and marketing documents should be updated regularly. I know some business owners who update their business and marketing plans daily and keep them open on their desktop or laptop every day of the week. Other business owners have their own way of regularly updating their plans.

What you are ultimately aiming for is to always have a profitable business plan. Sometimes you are going to need the courage of a lion, this is the best way I can describe preparing you for the road ahead. Times can be tricky; business events can go wrong. Allow yourself to stay strong and remain true to yourself.

At other times you will need to literally be the Ultimate warrior. Your stance and how you are laying your business foundations will strengthen you and strengthen your business too, so that your ascent is as smooth as possible, and your profits are well earned.

You will discover levels of determination in your character you had been blissfully unaware of until now that have been within you all along and are now at your fingertips to guide you along.

Running your own business can be invigorating, amazing and challenging. Keep up your persistence and determination. I have put these two words on every single page of every book in the "Business Mountain" series to encourage you.

Writing out your business plan before you start up your business can be a lot of fun and it helps you to clarify the structure of your business, making it ready to run in the most effective and efficient manner possible. Remember to stay true to you and never compromise yourself or your business at any time. This mantra should hold you and your business in good stead for the whole time you work on your business.

There are three main types of business plan. The first is generally a 4-page pullout of your main business plan.

In the military World this 4-page pullout is called the 'Generals & Admirals' in the U.K. it contains the basics of your business. There will be a sample of this pullout called the Chairman's & Managing Directors Summary in www.rabbitts.com/documents.

A ten or 20 page plan including 'Appendices' is fine for handing out to Investors and Shareholders when needed. Your long-term plan can be longer for your business's eyes only and can be as long as you like.

It is within the first three years of opening that a business is known to either succeed or fail. To shore up your business and to do your very best to prevent failure, creating your business planning ahead of launching can drive you and your business forward into profitability.

You may find "Naysayers" amongst your closest family and friends. Listen to them intently. Take on board any valuable warnings and discard any unnecessary criticism. You will be aware if things are going off the rails with your business, stay focused and diligent, and if things are not working well, ask for assistance where you need to and change it.

There could be many unexpected hurdles you have to find your way through for your business to find its feet. There will be things that you need to do that place you completely out of your comfort zone. Sometimes you are aware that these are things that none of your friends would be prepared to do. If they are true to you, get on with them anyway, as your biggest efforts produce the profitability you desire and the way of life you have dreamed of for yourself and those closest to you.

Uniqueness is worth pursuing, make your business the best it can be to your knowledge. Knowing what your customers want is half the battle. Giving them what you know they want comes next. The rest is work, and more work! When you are working for yourself in your own business, it can be incredibly exciting and thrilling as well. Its why you are doing what you are doing. This way of life is your way of life and your ascent up the "Business Mountain" will gradually get easier.

You may find plateaus along the way up your mountain, these are your celebration times. Make sure you celebrate the small victories along the way to the top, as holding off until you reach the summit until you crack open the bubbly will make if feel harder than it needs to be. Welcome your family, friends, advocates, and mentors to help you enjoy your achievements along the way too, keep your enthusiasm and focus up when the good times roll.

Lastly, remember there are business sharks around. You need to watch out for them and be always aware of them.

If they go unnoticed, they can bite hard which can often result in a financial loss along the way for you and your business.

When you start out you won't necessarily know what you want long term. A owner/family business or a way out (called an exit strategy. You don't need to know initially but keep in mind a way for your exit strategy should you want or need it. Discuss with your accountant, as necessary.

Remember the more time you work **ON** your business and not in the business the better. Now, if your business requires staff, they work **IN** the business only. You work **ON** the business... you will find yourself working in your business as well quite a lot but generally you'll need to be working on your business ...you'll know the difference.

Stay strong in your stance. Best wishes from me for your amazing business journey.

For
David, my 5 children and all grandchildren
and
my now Angel mentors
the two John's and Dennis.

"Shall I do it Den?"...
"Well, they can't hang
you for it Da!!"

Contents

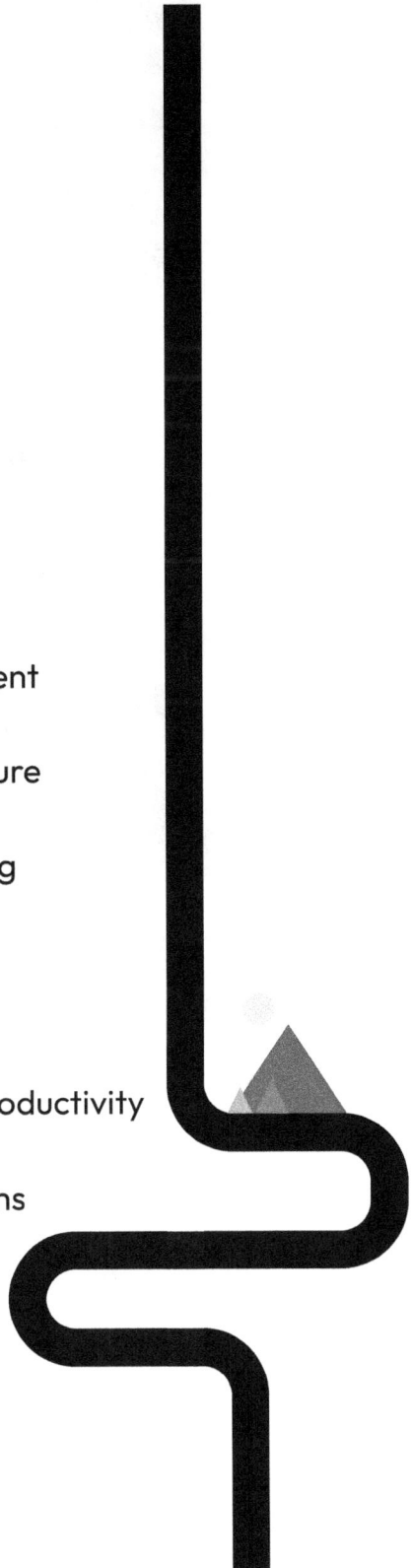

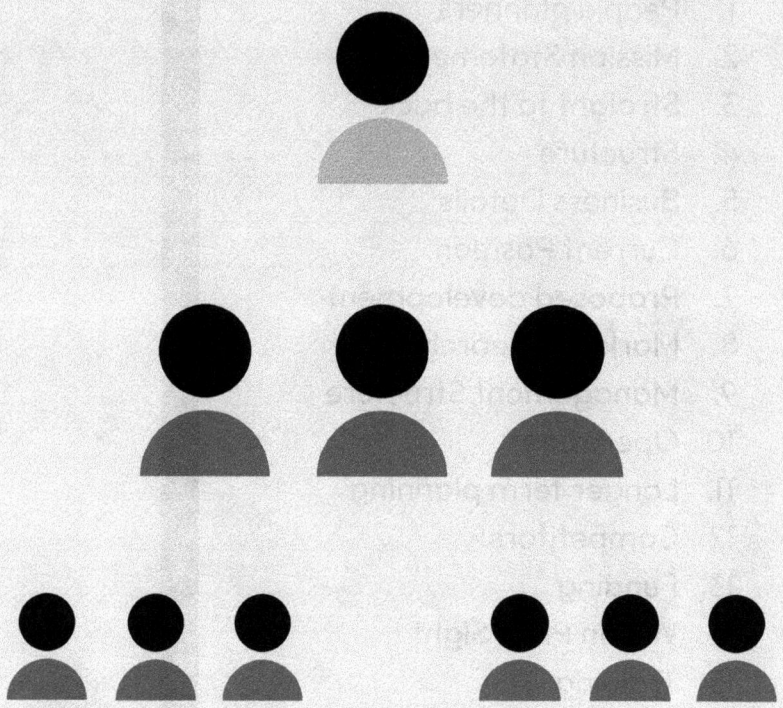

Chapter 1

PEOPLE PLANNERS

People planners

Who's gone here before us?

Hundreds and thousands of your fellow Countrymen/ women have trodden these boards, as they say in Theatre, before us.

Two in particular we remember very well.

Charlie Chaplain must have had immense Entrepreneurial flair like yourself.

He was born in 1889 into poverty in England and started performing from a young age. After moving to The United States of America in 1910 he worked as an actor in the silent films' era until in 1917. Chaplin decided to create his own studios. There is a picture of him with his spade in the heart of the residential section of Hollywood La Brea Avenue the now "Universal Studios".

1

Chaplin appeared to be experimenting with media and at the end of the War he made a film for the Government, which was used to popularise the Liberty Loan drive "The Bond". Then at the end of the war he created a film called "Shoulder Arms" which proved to be a veritable 'mirthquake' at the box office.

Even still today a going concern, Universal Studios still makes films but is also listed as part of the Orlando Florida Disney theme parks. Necessary changes have been made to keep up with the times. Also known as 'Change Management.' Now some Entrepreneurs become what is known as a stick in the mud. They won't allow their businesses to be changed as they have been doing it this way since the 1920's. So, they still have stock on their shelves from the 1920's !?! Do not let this be you. Assess the risks as carefully as you can. Move with the times when it is necessary. Try your best not to stay in the past with your business.

Another veritable "Entrepreneur" Selim Zilkha founded Mothercare in 1961. The Company grew fast and opened its 100th store in 1969.

Mothercare had been trading for many years. This photograph above is the one that was released when all the stores closed. Unfortunately, all businesses have a beginning a middle and an end. For the sixties, seventies, eighties and nineties, they must have been doing something right. In 2010 something must have changed in the World, and they maybe did not change their business model quickly enough.

They had been successfully establishing themselves as a household brand name and they had also successfully positioned the brand in the mind of consumers. The reason for choosing Mothercare over other brands is they had achieved the trust of their customers.

Trust is not just given by customers and over the years Mothercare worked to develop and maintain this trust.

Chapter 2

MISSION STATEMENT

Mission Statement

Let us gather our thoughts over **your mission statement** first. This is something you 'craft' for your business and all that you do. This statement that you create for your business forms the basis for your business.

It will be a noticeably short paragraph which explains the mission of your business.

Some other Companies Mission statements for you ...

'We will not lie; we will not cheat'.

ICI

'To accelerate the world's transition to sustainable energy'.

TESLA

'To be Earth's most customer-centric company, where customers can find and discover anything they might want to buy online, and endeavours to offer its customers the lowest possible prices'.

AMAZON

'Bring inspiration and innovation to every athlete in the world. *

*If you have a body, you are an athlete'.

NIKE

'Mothercare is the leading specialist retailer offering the widest range of clothing, hardware and toys for mother-to-be and young children (Mothercare.com)'

MOTHERCARE

'To produce amazing and innovative safety products that babies, children and adults will Love'.

SNUGGLESTIME

Now go think about the Business you already have or are about to start-up. What is your mission statement? What do you hope to achieve for your customers with your offering? How can you put that into one simplified sentence for your customers to know, to understand, to trust? Hone it down, keep it simple, say as few words as possible, make it mean it.... over to you...

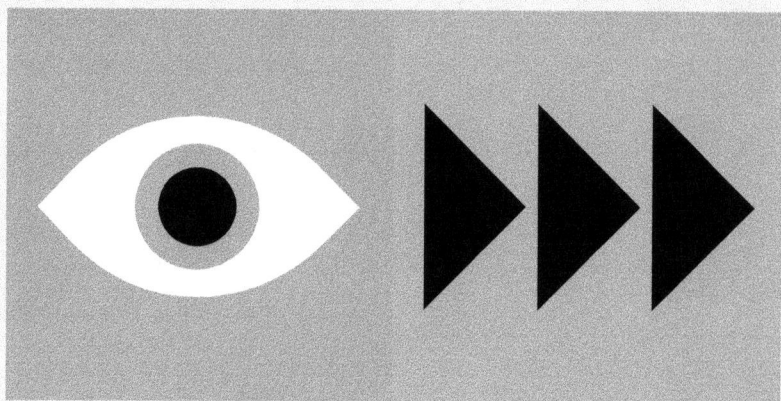

Chapter 3

STRAIGHT TO THE BACK

Straight to the back

When most professionals are handed a business plan, they will turn straight to the back of it, the last pages first. Just the same as if you pick up a book in a bookstore you will turn it over and read the back of it first. In both cases this is to find out what is going on with this document to hand. What is happening what are the financial components.

FINANCIAL SUMMARY

Here you do your chart of your 'current' finances.

I have set out below a typical current financial summary for you. You will need to do your own chart and list your own expenses etc.... Your accountant will be able to help you find all these figures. Your accountant may have all of this set out differently in an accounting software package for you. Or you can buy an accounting software package for yourself. The details below are to help you see the financial picture that a business portrays, and you can understand it in simple terms.

ACCOUNTS

It is worth noting here that it is easy to forget the dates by which you have to file your accounts with HMRC & with Companies House. You can check on Companies House for your Country.

Accounts - Fill this out & pin it up !

Date next accounts made up to ...../...../......

Date due by ....../........./......

Last accounts made up to ....../........./........

Confirmation Statement

Date next Statement date ...../....../......

Date due by ...../....../......

Last statement dated ...../........./........

Current

Year......................

£ ....Sales   £ ....

£ ....Less Purchases   £ ....

£ ....Carriage   £ ....

£ ....Packing materials   £ ....

£ ....   £ ....

                    Net Operating
£ ....Income (loss?)   £ ....

Administrative Expenses

Year................

£................Insurance   £................

£................Post and Stationery   £................

£................Telephones   £................

£................Broadband.................. £................

£................Sundry Expense   £................

£................Advertising/Marketing   £................

£................Training   £................

£................Motor expenses   £................

£................Entertaining, Travel,
Hotels & Subsistence   £................

£................Repairs & Renewals   £................

£................Legal & Professional Fees £................

£................Bank charges   £................

£................Depreciation   £................

£................Bad Debts   £................

£................Total Expenses   £................

£................Net Loss   £................

Balance sheet 31ˢᵗ Month..................... Year........

Assets
Fixed Assets

Year..................

£ ....Intangible   £ ....
£ ....Tangible fixed assets   £ ....

Current assets

£ ....Cash at bank   £ ....
£ ....Debtors   £ ....
£ ....Stocks   £ ....

Current liabilities

£ ....Other liabilities   £ ....
£ ....Loan from director   £ ....
£ ....Other liabilities   £ ....

£ ....   **Net current liabilities**   £ ....

Total assets less current liabilities

£ ....Funds   £ ....
£ ....Share Capital   £ ....
£ ....Profit & Loss Account   £ ....

Fixed Assets

	Intangible	Tangible	Total

Cost

	Intangible	Tangible	Total
Cost year/year	£	£	£ ....
Addition's year/year (E.g., All patents)	£	£	£ ....

DEPRECIATION 20% X Cost

	Intangible	Tangible	Total
20% Depreciation year/year	£	£	£ ....
20% Depreciation year/year	£	£	£ ....
	£	£	£ ....

Written down value

	Intangible	Tangible	Total
Net year/year	£	£	£ ....
Net year/year	£	£	£ ....

Chapter 4

STRUCTURE

Structure

'Your business name' Ltd to £1 (if Limited) in the name of (your ... name...) a 'your type of business' e.g., 'Marketing and Advertising Business'

Location: (your County, Country)

Address: (your 'business' address)

Company Registration Number: xyzxyz

You get this Company Registration Number from 'Companies House' in the U.K. Your accountant will be able to help you apply for this number or you can do it yourself on-line. Search up 'Companies House' on an online search engine. Go into the name checker to see if the name you want has already been registered.

'Gin's Tips'

If the Company name that you want to use is already in use by another Company, you will need to think of another Company name or use a variation of the name you originally wanted to use.

(Your title) 'E.g.,... General Manager Director' - (Your name)

U.K. based volume products manufacturer.

Manufacturers/Suppliers: list your manufacturers & Suppliers you are working with here.

Patents/Copyright/Design Registrations/Trademarks in (Your name)

One of "Gin's Tips"

I always make sure all patents/Copyright/Design Registrations are in my own name and are Licensed by myself to my businesses and are not put in the name of the Company. This way if the business gets into difficulties especially erroneous unforeseeable ones you do not lose your Intellectual Property with losing the Business.

License holder: (Your Initials only) (Your business's name)

How to create your own licence which you can get help with from a Licensing Practitioner or a Licensing Solicitor … will be in 'The Business Mountain' - Don't look down book (9) - Sales & Negotiations.

Purpose

(Your business name …) is a e.g., Sales and Marketing Company (Your product/service/shop/other)ranges.

(Your first name) has created designed the (Your product) - (e.g., 0-36 months) (your age range) which is the first product to be developed and this product alone has a potential (world-wide/local) sales value of £xyzzy, per annum.

This is where you put in your awards when you have entered any with your business or product or service and put them in if runner-up or nominated for and awarded as all these count for your Marketing and promotion of your business.

The (product/service) won British Invention of the Year Award 2002 & 2006 Bronze and Platinum – Consumer and various gold and silver design awards since.

With 20,000/(your figure) (products/service packages sold to date, the Volume Retail market across the UK will need to be approached and sales from the volume market will be used as a bottom-line to bring out the full range of potential (products/service packages).

So for instance you have sold ie. 20,000 units to your customers locally and this covers your 'bottom line or otherwise known in accounting as 'your break even' but the nationwide sales potential, now needs to be addressed.

Vision

(Your business name) has the potential to be a world/ county leading provider of xyz products/services for use by consumers, facilities, medical establishments, schools (have a think where your product/service can be used and who by and put it in here)

It can already be envisioned that a major UK company will grow from the innovative products/services to be brought out over the next 10 years and into the future under the Copyright/patents/design right/trademarks already granted by the UK Intellectual Property Office and on future products/services too.

We have engaged with our local MP so the local government representative is aware of the good work that we will be doing in this area of the UK.

'Gin's tips'

It can be worthwhile contacting your local MP and local Councillors so they are aware of the business that you are running that will benefit their constituents so they can bear you in mind and your business, when they come across information that may/or may not be of use to you in your business into the future.

Strategy

Have a think about how you want to strategize your own Business and write a paragraph about it here ... This will form the basis for why your business will gain it's customers.

An example for you ...

Through the disciplined application of a long-term business strategy. "Your business name" has the potential to increase revenues in the next (.... ?...... or 5years or decade) and we are confident in reaching (all local fish & chips eaters in this County and the adjoining ones - If opening for instance a fish & chip shop within the first few months) **or** (the majority of all 150 civilised Countries over the next 10 years - If a product to sell across the World)

The Company has the potential to (provide the best fish & chips at the best price so all locals know to head for our shop) or (be a world-leading provider of (xyz.. products - for (who or what type of person will your products be for !?!) E.g., Females, Retired couples, Consumers, facilities, medical establishments, and children).

The Company works in (for example - four main long-term target market(s) Nursery, Public Facilities, Medical, Toys and Books) Have a think which 1/2/3/4 main markets your business will be able to sell to !?! Write them down here under strategy of your Business.

1. Addressing (x) main markets

2. Investing in design, technology, capability, and Infrastructure.

3. Developing a portfolio of (products) or (services) or (more than one (x) shops)

4. Focusing on growing market share and install product/ service base/headquarters.

Cost

Initial funding to fund the formal launch of (your business name) – across the UK (your country) via Independent and website-based retailers (your outlets).

Forecast costs £xx,yyy See P&L forecasts.

The current RRP of the (Your product/service) is £xx. yy and can be sold/incentive (SOA's - Service orientated architecture) to £xx.yy by Supermarkets/Chain stores/

Volume Retailers..... Our own shop/our sales agents/our website.

The current manufacturing price is $xx.yy bagged up and ready to sell.

'Gin's Tips'

Prices are often quoted in dollars wherever you are in the world so be mindful of this and do not get your exchange rates mixed up.

Shipping from (Manufactured Country) is £xx.yy for a 20ft Container load and £xx.yy per product for a 40ft Container load.

It is worth keeping an eye out for yourself on the price of the petro-dollar. The price of crude oil in dollars on any one day. As this can affect all businesses if it changes in price drastically. Fuel economies and the manufacturing price of plastics and their product derivatives are dominated by the price of crude oil on any one day.

Chapter 5

BUSINESS DETAILS

Business Details

(Your Business name) needs to grow via sale to penetrate the U.K. market/County wide market with the (your product(s)/service) then gain access to the USA, European and all 150 civilized Countries.

Background

Due to the (x) years spent developing the market and preparing the foundations (your business name) is well positioned to gain volume sales entry points across the County/Your Country/The World. Taking this small company through to a medium sized U.K. company.

Evidence this in your appendices and financial forecasts.

(Your full name) currently works as/runs x Company and has experience in this this this and this.

(Your other employee's name) currently works as and has x years' experience in this this this and this.

List all other employees with their working attributes.

Features & Benefits

It's always best not to get your features and your benefits mixed up. Otherwise, you will make yourself look like a one-eyed bat from Venus especially to a potential Investor (If you ever want one, they are not necessarily an essential)

List your features only on an A4 sheet of paper and make sure they are **only features.**

Now do the same for the benefits for your product(s)

Here below I will set out for you the features and benefits of my baby safety product. This is so you know how to set out your features and benefits of your product(s)/service.

The features and benefits of this new product e.g. :

Features will be in normal script, benefits in italics:

·· A completely new restraining soft shoulder & waist harness to *prevent* ALL BABIES AND TODDLERS *escaping the changing mat and to prevent falls from high surfaces.* Giving peace of mind.

·· New Barrier Wall - *prevents fluids running off the end of the mat onto the surface you are changing baby upon (i.e., the bed or the carpet or adults' clothes)*

·· New Detachable Spoils Cloth. - *As long as a baby's clothes are beyond this cloth, its upper body clothes should not need to be changed if they wet during a change of nappy/diaper. This also helps to cope with a baby boy fountain. (Removed until turnover reaches over 1million mats)*

·· New Harness Adjustment. The mat design and easily adjustable soft harness provides for the child's own weight together with the rigid board to *ensure stability.*

·· New kneeling position on the Mat - *A more ergonomic design to allow adults to kneel on the floor to help prevent back strain from repeated nappy changing.*

" New thigh/ankle positions on the mat for parent / carer to sit astride the mat *for a more ergonomic and comfortable sitting position.*

" A new and much needed barrier wall to *prevent babies' clothes and parents' clothes getting wet during a nappy change. (Ergonomic : less washing, less electric, less washing powder, less drying)*

For use on the floor and on a high surface. Due to the ergonomic features. Babies and toddlers up to 36 months can have their nappies changed safely on the new Nappytime™ Changing mat.

Product Sales Plan foundation

There are a few things you need to find out here: -

Where are you planning to sell your product(s)/service?

Is it your own county only? Maybe a coffee shop? Or a kebab shop? A sewing clothes business? or a home decorating company?

An on-line clothing line/a safety training online service, whatever it is you have in mind, figure out the area & where the boundary lines are for your business. If it is in Herefordshire state that. If it throughout the world, the World, state that. If it is your village & your surrounding villages state that.

What is the age group of the people you will be selling to? Let us say you are going to create your own dog food go figure out the age group of the type of dogs you will be aiming at for sales. Is it puppy dog food? is it for elderly dogs? is it for all dogs? Is it mainly for German shepherd dogs?

Now there is a lot in here in this example to take in. If for instance you are going to make a dog food that is specialised for German Shepherd dogs this is called selling a unique or a niche product.

When you try to sell this type of niche product, you may run into retailer rejection as they may say to you "Your product is too niche for us". This doesn't affect your sales potential but it is just a 'Gin's tips' that this could happen to you. There are likely to be other retailers who welcome you with open arms. You can't win them all as the saying goes.

Getting back to the above we are trying to drill down into the age group of your potential customer.

Let us say you are going to create your own dog food. Go figure out the age group of the type of dogs you will be aiming at for sales. Consider which generation of owner you will be aiming at are they in their 30's, 40's .... 80's as they all buy differently. Is it puppy dog food?

Now elderly dogs are elderly for let us say their last 3/4 years. So, your customers could be 30 - 4 = 26 years of age. People own dogs right up to the age of what? Let us say 75 years of age.

So, for this example the age range of your customers is females and males from age 26 to 75 years of age.

This is an example of some mathematics you need to do for your business.

Now the market size for your business can be found from these figures.

How many 26- to 75-year-old females and males are there in the U.K.!?!

You should be able to find this out in the ONS website (ONS stands for Office of National Statistics)

On average 1 million babies are born across the U.K. every year half boys half girls generally.

So, to find out how many people there are in the age range you are looking at.

75 minus 26 = 49 multiplied by 1 million is 49 million potential customers …. THIS IS YOUR MARKET SIZE, but not all these people own dogs. Maybe 1 in 4 people own dogs.

So, your real market size is 1/4 of 49 million is 12 1/2 million. Sounds a bit more realistic? Good because it is.

Think all this through for your own business very very carefully and run it past your accountant too to make sure you are not inflating the figures. Not overestimating. Not exaggerating (It is common amongst Entrepreneurs to be over exaggerating… make sure you do not do it !!!)

I cannot express this enough that you must hold yourself back from exaggerating as it can prove to be your downfall!!!

If you overestimate the number of coffee drinkers in your county & you are opening a coffee shop, you could be way over-ordering your coffee beans for your shop to the point that they are out of date and have gone off before you have a chance to use them. Big mistake. This is so easy to do though. Forethought is what you need in your business. Try to see these mistakes before they happen, if you can.

Make it realistic, make it real, as it is likely to be then you will not be missing your target by a mile as they say.

Ok let us try again ..

Plan to sell (your product(s)/service) to 25% of the market size of 12.5 million owners of elderly dogs in the U.K, males and females, within 5 years, then plan to sell to all 150 countries within 10 years.

Once sufficient funds have been raised from sales of the (your product(s)/service), the next batch of products/ services will be created and released into the existing revenue streams.

Chapter 6

CURRENT POSITION

Current Position

(Xxxx) of (your product or service) have been sold to date.

Products have been designed so that they will fit on an 800mm x 600mm 1/2 size pallet and on a 1200mm x 1000mm sized standard pallet.

Basically, you need to know about pallets first. There are two main types a standard pallet and a half size pallet. Then there are blue pallets also. When you work with a Logistics company they will explain all of this to you too. A logistics company is one that has a warehouse full of pallets from lots of different customers. Let's say you have 20 pallets of stock created you would have it moved by a lorry to your Logistics company which will charge you per pallet for warehousing your stock on your pallets. Pallets are usually not stocked full any higher than 1500mm from the top of the pallet. Your retailers will have stipulated this measurement in their customer handbook for you. Each retailer has different rules, so you must be careful to meet the very specific criterions of your own retailer customers as you won't want your lorry turned away for not meeting all the criteria.

All pallets will be kept to a maximum height of 1500mm as this is normally the stipulated height for most retailers.

Let's say you are selling kettles. You will have each kettle boxed up in cardboard but then you will have a display unit created that has a certain number of kettles in it. Each pallet will then have a definitive number of your display units on it. Retailers will then bring these display units out onto their shop floors and your info branding will be all over the cardboard display unit(also known as a merchandising unit).

Now this is for anything you are likely to be selling: - Clothes, products,tools, you name it; it all boils down to the size of a pallet.

It is rather fortunate that I can warn you about this as the first products I had manufactured did not fit on a pallet!?! It was crazy. They overhung on the pallet, and they were all far too big. I had not honed them or back engineered them onto the standard size of pallet. I could hardly get any of my too big cartons onto a pallet.

This was one of my craters as I described in 'The Business Mountain' Don't look down - Book 1 for startups. I fell in it good and proper. Even ordered 2 40ft container loads and limped along with oversized stock. Until one day someone kindly said to me. "You're doing it wrong, do it this way".

Now my product cartons all fit neatly on their pallets and yours will too, I am sure.

Company x is selling my (x) product

Company y is selling my (x) product

Company z is using my product which gives us Marketing exposure.

At the end here of your 'Current Position', list your current customers and where they are coming from.

Let us say your Bed & Breakfast is about to open in Brighton U.K., overlooking the sea and you have put an advert in your local paper…

If you make your advert traceable, i.e., put a code on your advert that customers refer to, you will then know where certain customers are being generated from.

So, the B&B is getting booked up in advance by your customers and you haven't even opened yet.

Put e.g., local paper as the source of your customers here, then list your other sources of customers/your other Retailers.

Now I want you to have a good think about who your potential customers will be?

My baby changing mat is sold to consumers but can just as easily be sold to Restaurants, Hotels, Tourist attractions, pubs Hotels Tourist attractions pubs and hospitals etc. I created a Public Facilities version for this type of sale.

You now need to have a good think about who your customers will be.

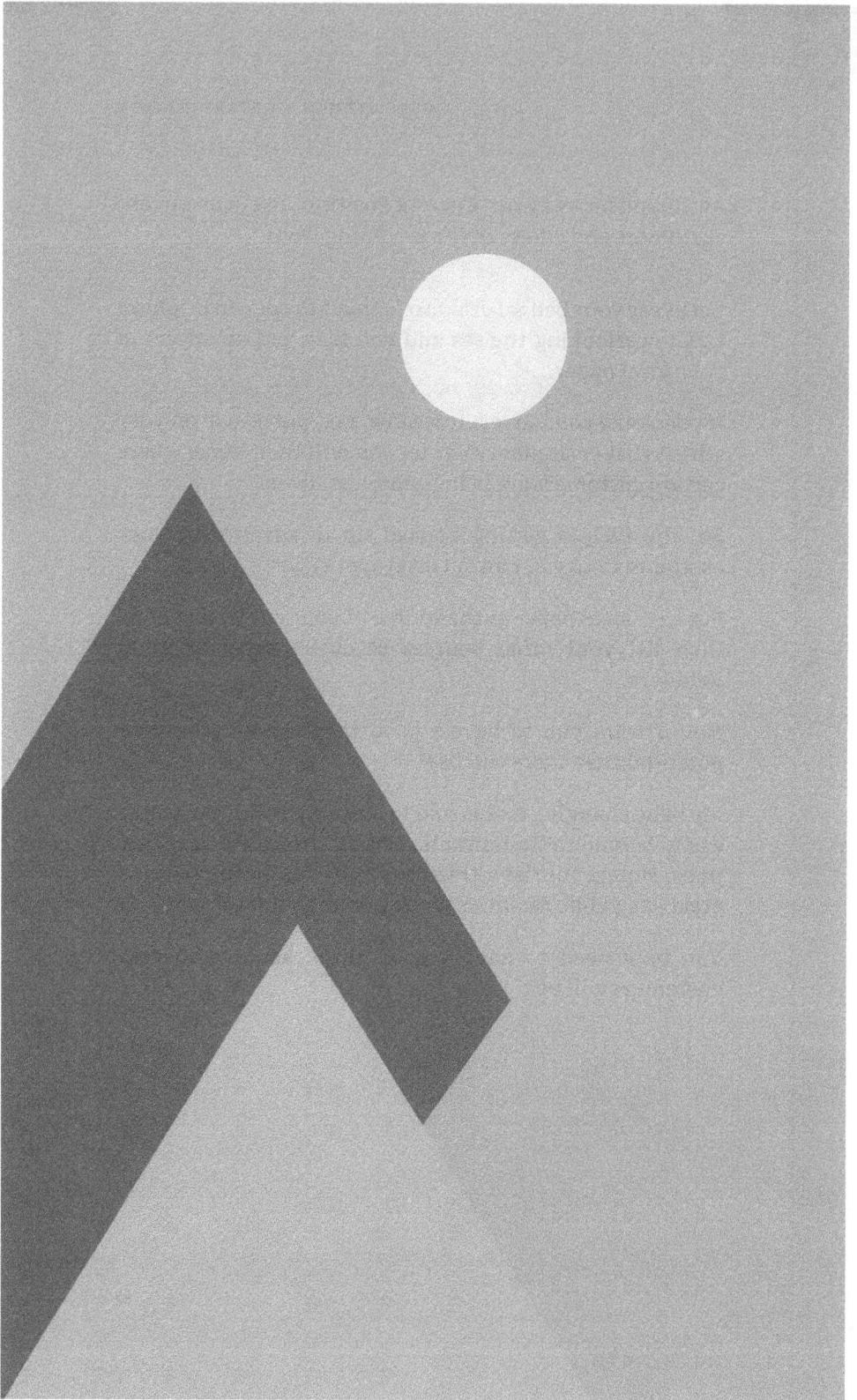

Chapter 7

PROPOSED DEVELOPMENT

Proposed development

Purpose of plan

The purpose of this business plan is to clearly set out the financial position for (your company name) in (year) and to lay the foundations for financial planning of the (your company name) collection of products for the future. (Pls note: - It's a good idea to produce a full marketing plan) A full 'Marketing Plan' is available upon request.

We will cover Marketing plans, which are entirely different to business plans, in 'The Business Mountain' Don't look down - Book 4 Marketing.

Potential products list

Here you list all your products that you plan to sell. If you plan to sell on-line training courses list them all here by their headings.

This will give you clarity over what business you are starting or continuing to shape up.

If you are selling products and you have accessories/add on's that will be sold too, list them here, after your main list of services.

If you will be running a hotel, list what you will be selling to your customers...

hotel rooms

Including soaps/shampoos/shower caps/sewing kits/ washed bedding/washed towels/fruit bowls/telephone service i.e. list of giftware, trips to events, beverages - Including wine, beer, coffee, milk, lemonade etc - food, Snacks.

Over the next 20 years (Your company name) plans to sell

1. Year 1 sell xyz
2. Year 2 sell xyz
3. Year 3 sell xyz
4. Year 4 sell xyz
5. Year 5 sell xyz
6. Year 6 sell xyz
7. Year 7 sell xyz
8. Year 8 sell xyz
9. Year 9 sell xyz
10. ... etc

Under each of these above xyz etc just list the names of the products/services you plan to sell no other details are needed for this outline.

S. W. O. T Analysis

Strengths

(Your Company name) is well placed to sell (your product(s)) in the U.K. as x,xxx,xxxx ??million people are born each year .... across the U.K.

Have a think about these figures which represent the number of people who are your relevant customers just to start with in the U.K.

Health Professionals/Doctors/judges of xyz award are all impressed by this product.

Have a think who is impressed by your product services, what professions are these people in ??

With many years (?) worth of planning and of putting in strong foundations (your company name) is well placed with many many contacts at our fingertips of (your company name) brand, creates great strength for (your business name) business growth into the future.

Weaknesses

(Your company name) has so many sales outlets that still need to be approached with the help of the funding required to properly launch the (your product(s) range into (your country)/other countries.

To overcome this lack of funding weakness the initial profits from sales of the products will be a great foundation to build upon.

Opportunities

(Your Company name) has proven in x outlets, there is Y potential stockists/sales/customers across the village/county/country (dependent upon your type of offering).

Threats

(Your company name) will need to keep a very good eye on its cash flow forecasting and actual cash flow as this is in the main the most obvious difficulty that besets young companies.

They are not aware enough of their CASHFLOW. Must keep a constant eye on CASH FLOW.

It would also be wise to know who your competitors are in your field and be aware of their marketing strategies. Best not to get too drawn in by your competitors though. Much better to do your own thing, get on with it doing it all your own way, taking only a cursory eye over what the competition is up to.

Risk

You can try to mitigate or lower your risks as much as you can, but here is an example of what you can be at the mercy of. For instance, if you own a vineyard in, let us say, the South of France, the weather can be very unpredictable ... waiting just one more week with the grapes can give a much better harvest, but can put the business at a massive risk of 1/2 or 1/3 output due to unpredictable weather conditions.

As explained in Book 1 for Startups, every business needs to prepare for the worst. What is called 'a war chest' is prepared .... Just in case business activity must be halted for long lengths of time, even over a year ... **big warning**. As many of us know, businesses can be hit by totally unexpected conditions. It is possible to prepare for these unknown conditions. See 'The Business Mountain Book 1 for Start-ups for more preparation details.

Chapter 8

MARKET RESEARCH

Market Research

Analysis of Research

This is where you list your market research efforts that have been carried out to date.

If you have already created your Market Research questionnaire as set out in the example in 'The Business Mountain' - Do not look down - Start-ups Book 1 and have carried out this research, then all your results get listed here. Also list the percentages of your results and the quirky revelations that this research revealed to you.

Here is the sample market research template (a) and (b)

SEE A SAMPLE QUESTIONNAIRE BELOW:

Questionnaire A

This is for Existing Mothers
1. With babies in buggies
2. Possible Mothers alone
3. Mum's with another adult

"IS THERE A CHANCE YOU COULD HELP ME? I AM DOING SOME MARKET RESEARCH INTO BABY PRODUCTS"

SHOW PHOTO (IF YOU CAN LEGALLY)

"THERE ARE ONLY 10 QUESTIONS, AND IT WILL TAKE LESS THAN TWO MINUTES OF YOUR TIME".

1a. May I ask you if you have any children?
If **yes**, then Qu **1b.**
If no, then '**thank you for your time**'.

1b. How many children do you have?

| 1 | 2 | 3 | 4 | Other | .... |

2. Did the changing mat that you bought for your first child last through all your children?

| Yes | No | ➡ | .... | N/A |

'*Why not?*'

Go to 8.

3. What condition is your most recently purchased Changing mat in?

| Poor | Good | V. Good | Other | .... |

4. Who chose the mat?

| I did | Someone Else | ➡ | .... |

State Relationship

Go to Qu. 7

5. Which shop/s did the changing mat/s come from?

....

6. Did you choose the mat because of

Colour	Pattern	Price	Size	Other

....

7. When your baby or babies became older, did you find the task of nappy changing?

Easier	Harder

....

Reasons why

8a. What surface did you use your mat on at home?

Bed	Changing Unit	Floor	Other

....

Specify

8b. Where are you usually in relation to the baby when changing a nappy?

At the side	At the end	Other

....

Specify

9. Have you ever experienced back pain from changing a nappy?

Yes	No

➡ ....

Details

10. What do you think of public changing facilities for babies?

....

Thank you very much for your valuable time. I need to ask at least 10% of people for their contact details to prove this research has been carried out. Is it possible to take yours ? Due to Data Protection GDPR all contact details will be destroyed once the research has been collated.

Questionnaire B

First time Mothers (Late Pregnancy)

"IS THERE A CHANCE YOU COULD HELP ME? I AM DOING SOME MARKET RESEARCH INTO BABY PRODUCTS"

SHOW PHOTO (IF YOU CAN LEGALLY)

"THERE ARE ONLY 10 QUESTIONS, AND IT WILL TAKE LESS THAN TWO MINUTES OF YOUR TIME".

1a. May I ask you if you have any children?
If **yes**, then **QUESTIONNAIRE A**
If no, then '**proceed**'.

2. Do you already have a baby changing mat?

| Yes | No | ➤ Go to Qu7. |

3. Did you buy the mat yourself?

| Yes | No | ➤ .... |

Who did?

4. Which shop did the changing mat come from?

....

5. Did you choose the mat because of

Colour	Pattern	Price	Size	Other

....

6. How much did you pay for the mat?

....

7. Do you know where you will be most likely to buy a changing mat from?

....

8. What will your decision be based on?

Colour	Pattern	Price	Size	Other

....

9. How much will you be prepared to pay for a changing mat?

....

Thank you very much for your valuable time.
I need to ask at least 10% of people for their
contact details to prove this research has been
carried out. Is it possible to take yours? Due to
Data Protection GDPR all contact details will be
destroyed once the research has been collated.

Once these answers are collated and we know hopefully at least 70% of people liked our idea then we can move forward to the planning stages.

To construct these questionnaires, you might have a good think around what you want to know about your offering, what sway of the purchase? Is it mainly the men who will be ordering/buying your product/service? Is it 60%Men 40% women or visa versa?

How many of those men are under 30? How many are over 30?

If you have entered your product/service into any competitions, put the results here. Did your product have more competition entries than any other competition entry for that xyz organisation that held it for you ? Put that here.

Was it 95% of the 1000 people who were happy for you to ask them the questions on your questionnaire ??

Your product/service has copyright, design registration, trademark registration and patent applications all in hand ... put the details of all these here.

Customers

The (your product/service) will be the platform for the small business leading to a medium sized Company.

The (your product/service) will be/is already in the marketplace and this can be replicated in our local village/ across the County of (your County)/across the U.K.

Word of mouth, logo branding, patents/copyright will be the foundations for sales stability and sustainable growth of the business.

As this is a new and exciting business ... free media coverage already obtained will be continued. As (your product/service) gains awareness, media coverage what works well with sales outlets county or country wide.

As (your product/service gains more Awards, the media will be sent press releases (See 'The Business Mountain' - Don't look down - Sales & Marketing Book 4 for construction of press releases).

The media need/like an invisible **'coat hook'** to hang your press info on. If your product has won an award or been nominated or made a runner up .. all of these are great invisible 'coat hooks' for the journalists & tv people to hang your information upon. Shhhh I didn't tell you this.

In a nutshell

For success products/ services ... should meet

THREE CRITERIA:-

(a) people must want the products of the business
(b) prices must be such like, so that people are prepared to pay
(c) the products must be known to those who want such things

The nature of the business and product(s) is such that it can be flexible, and the business is able to develop in new directions, when appropriate. Close contact with the 'market' will enable the business to stay in touch.

The 2020 Covid19 crisis has been a major example of how businesses must diversify themselves, be flexible, and change with the times.

Many of the large chains of pubs and hotels had shored up their businesses ready for this business interruption, as it is called. They made sure over the years that they had gradually bought all the freeholds under all their properties. So, when there no income for over a year for all the, in some cases over 600, businesses, there was also ... no property rent to pay.

Then when you have a property portfolio, there will be some of your properties that will be worth a 'darn sight more' as they used to say.

To sell one of these properties would then shore up the remaining businesses, to the tune of 200 million in some cases for a Capital city/London U.K. property. Levelling out the business generally ... so the staff and the business can be protected (Keeping it afloat)

This is another example of the business war-chest, as described in 'The Business Mountain' - Book 1 - Start-ups.

Potential customers

List them here ...

Who will you have the potential to sell to?

These would be your potential customers, customers that you could potentially sell to if you've got your act together & made yourself fit with their businesses.

Have a good think about who your product/service is designed for as an end point of sale, and which stores wholesalers could you potentially sell to.

1. Online store 1
2. Online store 2
3. Direct through own website
4. Via sales agents to xyz
5. If a pub, to pub goers over 18/families/elderly/ workmen/women

6. If a safety course, to care homes/factories/NHS/.....

7. If to major retailers, list them

8. If a sweet shop, to consumers/care homes/hotels/?/?

9. X - Store 200 stores (Your Country)

10. Y - Store 5,700 stores worldwide

11. Z - Store 10,000 stores Europe

Drawing up this list is one thing ... making it happen for your business is quite another.

Help as to how to go about selling to a variety of customers you will find in 'The Business Mountain' - Sales & Negotiation Book (9)

Potential consumers

Here you may find you have an extensive list of potential consumers... here is mine for you to help you write your list.

·   Young pregnant girls 16-20

·   Pregnant women 21-25

·   Pregnant women 26-30

·   Pregnant women 31-45

·   Mothers of a new-born baby

·   Mothers of 1 baby (3 months old)

·   Mothers of 1 baby (6 months old)

·   Mothers of 1 baby (9 months old)

·   Mothers of 1 baby (12 months old)

- Mothers of 1 baby (18 months old)
- Mothers of 1 baby & pregnant with second
- Mothers of 2 babies
- Mothers of 2+ babies
- Dads
- Grandparents
- Child-Minders
- Health Visitors for use in Baby Weighing Clinics.
- Hospitals for children's wards/casualty/outpatients
- Midwives to use in clinics
- Grandparents
- Nannies or Employers of
- Aunties & Uncles
- Nursery's
- Midwives
- Doctors
- Children's wards
- Maternity wards
- Disabled parents
- Parents of disabled children
- Hotels/ships/shopping centres/Tourist attractions/museums/churches/
- Restaurants
- Public Facilities

- Those who wish to impress others with their possessions.
- Those who aim to purchase anything and everything new and or available for their infant, especially all safety products that are available
- Initially those consumers who are always the first customers of newly launched products (Early birds)
- Those who have babies who are perpetually attempting to escape their existing changing mat
- Those who work in professional jobs where they must wear smart clothes, which they need to prevent from being soiled and who would still like to do the last change before they leave for work.
- Those who must change several nappies for a variety of children in the course of their working day i.e., nannies in nurseries, crèches etc... child minders.
- For the baby list that pregnant mothers write up before the birth of their baby and then proceed to purchase.
- As a fashion accessory 'like Messenger handbags'
- Ambulances

Competitors

Competition in all industries comes in many forms, each presenting different competitive situations for you.

With your business on the playing field as they say your competitors may up their advertising and lower their prices.

It is best to only have a cursory eye over what others are doing and just do your business your way. Put your invisible business blinkers on, just like the racehorses have on at the start of a horse race. This will prevent you from becoming distracted by what others are doing.

When you have created a patentable product, you may get others circumventing your product, making very similar products to yours. You may be prepared to sue any infringers of your patent directly equating to the amount of turnover involved and consider business insurance, sometimes called patent insurance.

We at (your business name) will actively sue any perpetrators of copying products through the courts, equivalent to the turnover of the whole project offending business, the maximum damages and legal costs.

Small producers of similar products will be monitored...

Foreign producers ... present the greatest of competition. Full and powerful branding and appropriate logos, copyrights, patents, trademarks, and design rights will be used to deter foreign copying.

When approaching foreign manufacturers, it is worth finding out from them if they have already worked with any British or businesses from your own Country. If they have, this is a good sign for trust, as they wouldn't want to ruin their existing connections with their past and current customers, so they would be more unlikely to just go off and copy your offering.

Chapter 9

MANAGEMENT STRUCTURE

Initial management structure plan

Key personnel

Management team (CVs supplied)

——-

Make sure you create Curriculum Vitaes for all personnel. There are many many ways of creating a CV. I have set out two of the great ways of setting out a CV for yourself or for your key employees. These CVs need to be kept up to date regularly. It is fine to create your CV however you want it to be as there is no right or wrong way, but it must be clear, concise and compact, not lengthy. Two A4 pages is sufficient.

CV example 1 here...

(Your name)
Your

(Your address)
Photo

(Your address)

(Your address)

(Your postcode)

(Your mobile number)

(Your E-Mail address)

Profile

Here you give a few sentences about yourself and your working life. Keep it short succinct and to the point.

Experience

- Here you bullet point your working life experiences
- Put your most recent working experience at the top
- Then write down all or most of the other types
- Of working experience (One sentence that you have had in the past, or just those relevant to your business venture).

Work experience

2021 - date (Your job title/(s)) . Company you're working for

2006 - 2021 (Your job title/(s) Company

1989 - 2006 (Your job title/(s). Company

You do not have to list all your jobs here ... 'horses for courses' so put all of them on, or just the ones you see as relevant ones.

Education

Put in here only what you deem to be relevant... you don't have to put all education in here.

1989 - 1991 XYZ

Personal details

Nationality: British !?!   Official secrets act signed:
x/y/2056

Status: Married/single/etc Born: (your DoB)

Good working knowledge of: xyz languages

Driving licence: Full clean & current

Directorships/Judge/Awards

- List here any relevant awards
- Any Directorships current and past
- If you have been a judge at an exhibition or competitions

Activities and Interests

In your everyday life what are your hobbies and or interests … just one or at the most two lines here …

Use triple words here e.g. honest, reliable, trustworthy

Hardworking, approachable, friendly

Go on, describe yourself in your best image.

Business course accredited

- Here list all the business courses you have been on

Software package awareness

- Here list all the computer courses you have been on/ are competent with.

CV example 2 here .....

(Name)(middle names)(Surname)

(Your town) (Your county)

(Your E-Mail address)/(Your mobile)

Curriculum Vitae

A paragraph about yourself

I am ..

I have .....

I want to ....

I also want to ...

Use triple words here honest reliable trustworthy

Hardworking approachable friendly

Go on describe yourself in your best image.

Work placement/experience

February 2056 Ongoing **Job title - xyz** job for jkl Company Working in xyz

April 2050 to February 2056 **Job title** - abc job for def Company

Working in xyz

September 2045 to 2050 **Job title** - vwx job for uvw Company

Working in xyz

Qualifications

2040 these qualifications

2038 these qualifications

College

2033 these qualifications

Interests & Additional Skills

Put your abilities and individual skills in here

Full clean driving licence (Only if you have this)

References available upon request

These CVs are put at the back of your Business Plan under your 'Appendices'

Management team (CVs supplied)

General Manager, Director: (Your name)

Sales & Marketing Director: (whose name ?)

Facilities & Quality Assurance: (whose name ?)

Now list all the Companies that you will be working with. There are some examples below :-

The following will provide support and assistance:

Accountants:

Insurance Agents:

Solicitors:

Patent Attorney:

Shipping Agents:

Logistics & Warehousing:

Designers:

Website hosting:

Website purchase:

Website designer:

Printing Graphics Designer:

Trade Association:

Advertising PR & Marketing:

Personnel Consultant:

Various Family Members:

Business Mentors:

Skills Analysis

Managing Director

(Your name) will operate the business (initially). (Your name) has had many years' experience/ is fully competent/ trained in xyz. (Your name) also has the following a b & c skills which will support the business through to profitability.

Recruitment

All staff can be recruited by (Your name) with assistance from (your human resources consultant … if you need one) or recruitment agency (x).

Chapter 10

OPERATIONS

Staff issues

All staff issues will be the responsibility of the General Managing Director.

With help from:-

- Local Enterprise Agency (name)
- Chambers of Commerce (Area)
- The Company/Employee Law Directory
- Personnel Consultant (name)
- Solicitors

Production procedures/Service processes

All production/processes will be controlled by the following:-

- (Your Business name) procedures
- (Your Business name) specifications
- Official Drawings
- British Standards Institution
- Trading Standards Institution
- European Standards
- Australian Standards
- U.S.A. Standards (Find this name Gin)

- HOKLAS Certificates (**Important**:- If manufacturers are in China - must be pre-production Certification)

- (Your Business Name) Quality Documentation

- All other (Your Business name) Official documentation

Premises

(Your Business name) will operate from ..... xyz address.

With logistics warehousing at abc address

All suppliers will be sourced in-house, and supplies will be controlled by (your Business name) to ensure best quality and best prices.

Purchase/Stock control

All purchasing will be continued via the (your Business name) purchasing/record keeping procedures as have been set up.

Here you will need to have created your own Purchase Invoice format and your own Invoicing format.

See below some sample format's for both these documents.

You can create these documents in any A4 word processing software, or your software based 'accounting package' may generate these for you. It depends how you want to portray your Business, but these methods can be too boring and miss a trick on long term memory of your customers.

Or you can do as I do and have a graphics designer create a document for you with all your logos and branding on both documents, memorable, clear-cut, defined, refined to your specifications.

With both your business invoices and purchase invoices there is something here to be aware of.

The numbering of your Invoices where you are Invoicing your customers. There is a real temptation to start with number 1 and make the next customer number 2. Please be careful of doing this as if you do this and each of your customers pays let's say £2,600 per invoice.

When you get to your 1000th invoice the invoice number will be 1000 but all your customers will know your turnover

is £2,600 x 1000 = £2,600,000

Be very careful of doing this as your turnover is meant to be and should remain entirely private.

If anyone ever asks you about the financial side of your business, keep it to yourself, just say my accountants wouldn't be happy for me to discuss this information as accountants know that financials remain private.

A better way of constructing your invoice numbers is :-

(Your company initials)(today's date)(sale type code)(some set numbers)(serial numbers)

Eg:

SDL12042021495550004

This way your customers and your staff for that matter, will be blissfully unaware of your turnover.

Subcontractors

All subcontractors and their subcontractors will have been assessed for :-

- Quality (ISO 2003 & ?????) or equivalent reliability. (This ISO number changes with time so you will need to look up the current ISO legislation)

- Specification Certificates required on goods for sale from their companies to meet BSI requirements laid down for all (your business name) requirements.

- Each Company where necessary will be Licensed to provide goods to (your company name).

- References will be taken up in each instance.

- Health & Safety policies.

- Valid necessary insurance certificates (copied)

- An official exchange of letters between each Company and (your Company name) will be recorded

- A Memorandum of Understanding with each Company will be exchanged with (your Company name)

- A confidentiality agreement with each Company will be exchanged with (your Company name) where necessary.

- A non-disclosure agreement with each Company will be exchanged with (your Company name) in all instances.

Below I have set out for you samples of the following documents:-

- Memorandum of Understanding

- Non-disclosure Agreement

These below are sample documents only. You will need to ensure any Legal requirements for the industry you will be working in are reflected in these documents. Any business Solicitors will be able to help you with this.

Non-disclosure Agreement

Parties to the agreement

Name:..............................Company:.............................

Address:...

....

....

TEL:-

FAX:-

MB:-

Name:..............................Company:.............................

Address:...

....

....

TEL:-

FAX:-

MB:-

Subject to formal contract basis of agreement

On the understanding that both parties are interested in meeting to consider possible collaboration in developments arising from (your name) Intellectual property including his/ her (patents)(patents pending) (copyright) It is agreed that the information, documents and materials supplied in the course and as a result of so meeting will be confidential.

This confidentiality applies to both technical and commercial information which either party may communicate to the other.

Excepted from this undertaking of confidentiality is any information in the public domain or which the receiving party can show was already in his/her/their possession prior to its disclosure.

Either party to this agreement shall on request from the other return forthwith any documents or items connected with the disclosure and shall not retain any unauthorised copies or likeness.

After 5 years from the date hereof each party shall be relieved of all obligations under this agreement.

....

Date...

(YOUR NAME)..

(YOUR SIGNATURE) ....

....

Date ....

(Chairman's name ....

(Chairman's signature ....

Memorandum of understanding

(Your name) Your Logo

Your address

....

....

....

TEL: ....

FAX: ....

MB: ....

E-mail ....

Websites: ....

Contact name ....

Company ....

Company Address ....

....

....

TEL: ....

FAX: ....

MB: ....

E-mail ....

Websites: ....

Company staff contact(s): ....

....

I am pleased to confirm a memorandum of understanding between myself and the company as mentioned above. On the understanding that both parties are interested in starting to consider possible collaboration in developments arising from (your name's) (Intellectual property)/(Copyright) including (his)/(her) patents or patents pending it is agreed that the information, documents, and material supplied in the course and as a result of so meeting shall be **confidential.**

Signed on behalf of:-

(Your Company name)..

(Your Company number)..

(Your signature) ....

....

Chapter 11

LONGER TERM PLANNING

Marketing/Publicity/Communications/Sales

All the chapters above can be included in your 20-page general Business Plan.

Now we go on to look in a little more depth at the other components of your longer-term Business Plan. Your long-term business plan can be set over 10 years 15 even 20 years.

Some business owners keep their business plan close to their chest, as it were, so it will always be open on their desktop or laptop and they will edit it daily. Others weekly ... some have no plan, they just get on with it. Others set it all up and just adhere to it, making a few tweaks/changes along the way. This all depends on the type of person you are, if you like and are familiar with documenting and planning .... It has been known for a few individuals to rather incredulously, put their whole business plan on the back of a beermat .... Yes this has been done many a time .. again it depends on the type of person you are and the type of business you are running ....

'To fail to plan is to plan to fail' .... We must all **plan.**

Marketing

To be adhered to in conjunction with the Marketing Plan document number

(i.e. your business name initials 000x)

A marketing plan is set out for you in The Business Mountain - 'Don't look down' Book (4)

Below is a basic outline of the marketing practices that you can/could/will apply to your business.

The marketing of the products/service will be made upon the principal benefits of the invention/product(s)/service idea itself. It will be certain and particular xyz safety/enhanced/new/novel attributes and how the business operates and the business's service idea's ability to make life easier/new/different.

As is the purpose of many a business/invention.

The output of the product/service to sell requires the *faith and the belief* of the potential customers - the psychological acceptance of some (post manufacturing effects/service implications and benefits. If a credibility gap opens up, there will be additional problems to resolve. Quite apart from the main objective of vast sales/great sales/steady sales/your words each year (e.g., ...as 780,000 babies are born every years/as there are 7,000,000 teenagers.... justify here using the stats that apply to your customer group)

The product/Service must justify the faith placed by the customer in the maker.

We should aim for pre-sale/pre-order anticipation followed by post-sale justification, and resultant recommendation, generated.

We will generate a considerable element of trust in order to build a relationship with potential or actual customers provided. They will only be content when they are confident that their needs appear to be fulfilled.

Winning the confidence of individuals through high quality education, communication and information will be an essential ingredient of the marketing.

These products/this service will be submitted to xyz television program for broadcasting ... E.g. at the end of the year/ at the beginning of the year 2056. Trends in the market and in demand upon the business may determine further development of the product(s)/service and customer service.

It is worth noting here that it is not always necessary to 'gold-plate' everything in your business. If your customers are plenty in numbers who use your facilities let's say you own a fitness gym. It does not necessarily need to be perfect all the time. If a wall needs painting as it is starting to look faded or unsightly, but you are still running at capacity in your gym then do not fret. Take the time that is needed to get to all the jobs that need doing in your business. If the business doesn't suffer as a result. Then just keep going forward with it.

If, however you own hotel and some of your rooms are in such a bad condition your customers would not return and more importantly they would not recommend your hotel.... then you will need to redress this swiftly.

In the age of social media, the reporting apps where your customers give feedback as to the quality and worthiness of your offering. We go back to ... be the best you can, do the best job you can ... **never ever compromise yourself nor your business** (live by this).

Remember, your Business is only as good as your worst review. So, raise the bar with your business. Exceed your customers expectations. Win your customers. Also bear in mind your competitors may write you a bad review.

There is an old saying isn't there from the past ... 'The customer is always right' In the restaurant/hotel trade this makes us laugh & we say "The customer can be right, but not always"

You can object to bad reviews on whichever medium, and you can demand they are removed. Check your rights at the time & politely sort it out.

If we do get given a review which we know to be unfair/ unjustified make sure you make efforts to have it removed if at all possible before it damages your future business.

For success, products/service must meet 3 criteria :-

1. People must want the product(s)service of the business

2. Prices must be such that people are prepared to pay

3. The products must become known to those who want such things

The nature of the business and product(s)/service is such that it will be flexible and able to develop in new directions, if appropriate. Close contact with the '*market*' will enable the business to '*keep in touch*'.

Marketing ploys:-

Here list the types of marketing ploys that you plan to create ..... and list the reasons why your customers are likely to want what you are offering...

Here are some of my ploys for the marketing of my baby safety products and some of my potential customers reasonings.

Reasonings....

- Those who wish to impress others with their possessions.

- Those who aim to purchase anything and everything new and or available for their treasured child.

- Initially those who regularly product early bird.

- Those who have babies, which are perpetually attempting to escape their existing changing, mat.

- Those who work in professional jobs where they must wear smart clothes, which they need to prevent, from being soiled but they would still like to do the last change before they leave for work.

- Those who must change several nappies for a variety of children in the course of their working day i.e., nannies in nursery's crèche's etc....child minders.

There may be seasonal activity at Christmas time, and possibly in certain months of the year, this will need early orders and planning.

(Your Company) will produce a formal Marketing plan in conjunction with a marketing questionnaire, which will have produced results by Year_____(complete).

Marketing ploy's....

1) Word of mouth

2) Leaflets

3) Adverts

4) Advertorials

5) TV news broadcasts

6) TV programs

7) Safety posters

8) Social Media funnel marketing

9) Blogger competitions

10) Blogger info output

11) Daily Social Media posts

12) Website

These are the ploys that I applied to my business and more.

There are over 150 different & separate general marketing ploys that we can all use and there are also now a good 150 social media and Website's marketing ploys to use in addition to the traditional 150 marketing ploy foundations that were available in the old days and still are available today.

Some of the ploys that I have listed here for you proved to be immensely powerful for my business.

This is a 'horses for courses' type of notion going on here though. So, some of these ploys I used will be no good at all for your business as they would be inappropriate for the business that you are running.

We all need to remember though with all these marketing ploys '*word of mouth*' *always* comes out top of the list as the best way to let your customers know your business exists. But I would have to say, social media funnel marketing must now come a close second.

Marketing needs to be tailored to each specific business.

Imagine a long plank of wood and it is held up by 10 individual wooden struts. Each strut is one of your marketing ploys holding the long plank (your marketing) up.

As you try out other different marketing ploys, knock the ones out of the way that don't work. Once you have found the best 10 marketing ploys for your business, they should be able to support your business into **profit**ability into the future.

Word of mouth statistically gives '**the**' highest marketing return.

Communications

Communications are of paramount importance. The need to communicate a message of a quality business conveyed succinctly, carefully and honed must be done appropriately.

We as business owners can be the ones with the knowledge of how peoples' lives can be more fun, easier, simpler, enriched, bettered. It is down to us to communicate what is better about life when people become our customers. For a lot of businesses, we can make them

· Charming

· Organised

· Beautiful

· Relaxing

· Comfortable

· Amazing even

So, you want to open your own barbers' shop in a ccertain high street. Where do you want to shop? At the end of the high street away from a very well-established barbers or right next door or as near to the very well-established business. **Do not** ever be afraid of the competition. In this instance, your shop is full of customers because you have 'upped your game', your shop front is amazing and inside is stunning to a point.... when potential customers are walking past both businesses which one are they going to choose?? Where are they going to go?? You have got this my friend, you've got this.

It doe not matter if we want to make a business of long dresses, so we think to ourselves how can I do that? Long dresses are made by hundreds of companies? You simply do it 'your' way, have the edge your way, and do not look at how anyone else does it. Be your own man. Be your own woman. **Be yourself.**

When you have a service, it is all about the people running the service, paying attention to detail, having foresight, anticipating the needs of our customers, and exceeding their expectations but and it is a big '**BUT**'! **ALWAYS** within budget!

Many a restaurant has fallen foul of this, giving so much food on the plate the customers cannot manage it all and they are all seen leaving the premises with doggy bags .... Know and remember that is your *'profits'* walking out the door in those doggie bags.

Your customers at this point, do or may not know or understand that you have this amazing device or an innovative way to overcome a difficulty, that you have solved for them. To overcome any misunderstanding, you must be able to communicate clearly. You must be able to convey exactly the information required, so people understand perfectly and engage with you and your product.

Your website, if you decide to have one, will be your business's window to the world. Websites, when they are constructed properly, will convey in the best manner what you are selling, and it will make it clear how your customers can buy your product or service from your business. Think of the products and businesses you love enjoy trust and are impressed by. Now go look at their websites. The major companies will spend over £1 million on their websites. It is good to see what they have included. When you find a website designer, you can get quotes for the type of site that you know your business needs.

It is worth knowing.... You will buy your website address/ domain name from a website seller then you will need to find a website hosting company to host your site for you. There are many companies that sell websites/domain names and there are many hosting companies too.

Once you have your website up and running you can take a peek at a fair amount of invaluable information about how your website is working for you. 'Analytics' are often provided by your website hosting company or by the search engine companies. You can then check out what type of traffic is looking at your site which country they are in, how long they were looking at your site for and whether they looked at your site on the first page only & then left your site or read your other pages. There are hundreds if intricate data information that may help you improve your business and improve your website and it may help you understand the general nature of your business.

It will be important to become known by **reputation** as well as by advertising. The successful communication of the product(s)/service will happen by creating an amazing service or bright colourful exciting & *new* quality manufactured product(s).

The Business/manufacturing operation should be efficient including all administrative systems which will be modern and appear to be so. This will create a favourable impression with individuals and help to minimise administrative processes.

Here ... you will need to make sure all your administrative processes are streamlined. If you can afford to delegate and employ others to do your administrative processes, do it.

You can also hire a virtual assistant to do all the more menial tasks like regular social media posting, handling emails and other areas of administration you require help with.

You do need to keep reminding yourself that you **need to work on the business** and not so much **in the business** unless your skills are the business.

You can find yourself being what I call a 'busy fool' spending 80% of your time doing admin and HR.

Production and time schedules should be computerised for accuracy and speed of issue. A delayed delivery to a retailer or a tutor who fails to turn up will be a loss of sales. If you under supply or fail to supply, you are likely to lose customers. Planning and forecasting can help to prevent this type of business hiccup and, if these hiccups cause any necessary wastage, you can build in planned limiters to prevent this. Non-productive hours will need to be minimised to gain maximum **profitability.**

When communicating, remember people will tell 5 people something good & they will tell 11 people about something bad.

If you are careful, you can use this knowledge. This can be done by making your audiences'/listeners/potential customers jaws drop. Tell them something they won't forget.

Accounting and costing of manufacturing/business operations will be computerised for the same reason..... **profitability.**

The ideal would be to have a 'bulk order book'/ advanced service bookings diary of set quantities of the products produced to a weekly production schedule. Thus, ensuring maximum utilisation of manufacturing facilities and productivity. This can be built upon alongside direct sales straight from the business apps and websites.

Easy accessibility to the business headquarters for potential customers will enhance the opportunity for sales. Personal contact will be a key feature of marketing, promotion and selling by the founder of the business until if it is necessary the board of Directors take over the running of the business.

Publicity

Making the business known to the people who will buy from us may be accomplished by:-

- Opening an intriguing countdown website

- Spreading reputation by recommendation

- Public relations strategy campaign - slowly telling the public to be aware of your product or service in the relevant locations for your offering.

- Approach journalists/news media, for your location with a press release or e-mails all consistent with any tv broadcasting.

- Take stands at appropriate trade and consumer exhibitions. Enter judging m competitions. If you win awards, or become a runner-up send a press release and alert journalists by e-mails.

- Advertorials

- Tick-lists with subsequent mail-shots in magazines.

- Advertising

- Banner and side panel website adverts

- In app advertising for your chosen Social Media sites

For a service type business, incentive promotions you can create and special packages you can create too.

Providing hotel rooms rates and food and beverage only. Would likely only be picking up a fraction of the potential turnover as day trips special events and all manner of other options for your customers can be tapped into. To the point that only 20% of the revenue from your customers is their stay in their room & the other 80% of their bill is the add-ons that you are providing.

- All the above will only be **considered** once the business has been launched on ... I.e. , 21st May 2056 ... and the business xyz insurance policies are all in place (for that date).

Advertising could be taken with the following organisations to make our best attempt at finding this product(s) services best advert outlet.

- In all appropriate journals :- online and hardcopies

- In all local papers:- online, social media, hard copies

- Using the tick system operated by the magazines for competitions polls and questionnaires, banner adds & side panel ads, adverts & advertorials.

- In trade appropriate magazines

- In alternative journals such inflight magazines, health magazines etc...

Now I will list the types of Exhibitions that I would be attending in my field of business... so you can see there is some diversity here to look out for ...

You will need to go find out, then write your list of appropriate exhibitions you can attend with your product(s)/service

Consumer Exhibitions (there can be large and small versions, try seeking them out)

Trade Exhibitions (Hopefully there is at least one trade exhibition for your field/sector)

Professionals' exhibitions (most of the professionals have their own exhibitions)

Disability Exhibitions

Invention exhibitions

European and USA exhibitions for all the above

World-wide exhibitions for your product(s) service.

1. leafleting, brochure poster distribution

(Think where your smart posters could all be put up ... if posters are good for your business)

2. Include professionals in the knowledge use of product(s)/service

Spectacular packaging branding – business status

Press releases/product photographs, business videos business specific and drone aerial footage portfolio showing initial concept of product(s) services.

Links, reels, stories, and posts personally too on social media with the right number of characters and hashtags permitted per post reel or story as appropriate.

Who these can be sent to/approached with:-

1. Certain TV programs

2. Friends

3. Acquaintances

4. Advocates (people who really believe in you)

5. Your e-mail list with special regard for GDPR (check out mailing apps)

6. Professional trade bodies

7. Business outlets specific to your business.

8. Direct marketing agencies.

9. National newspapers

10. Which magazine

11. Shopping channels

12. Specific tv inclusive programs ... i.e.: competition programs.

13. Product placement tv programs (maybe a soap tv program to show your product being used)

14. Mail order catalogues

15. Online sales outlets

16. Social media sales outlets

17. Social media adverts

18. Social media banner adds

19. Social media side panel ads

20. Social media reels

21. Social media stories

22. Social media videos

23. The sheds (Department Stores, Major retailers)

PRESS RELEASE!

Wednesday 4 October 2017

Introducing the award winning

NappyTime™
Changing Mat

Easier.
Cleaner.
Safer.

A simple idea that has completely removed the stress of the nappy change. Nappy changes can become a nightmare with a baby who constantly rolls out of your grip and crawls away no matter what state their bottom is in. The NappyTime™ Changing Mat eliminates this problem with its 'Special Harness' and ridged board inside which gently and safely keep your child from rolling away and escaping during a nappy change.

A shocking number of babies fall from a high surface every day and end up in A&E and go on to require hospital treatment for a multitude of injuries. This product can and does prevent injury. A stressful experience at the best of times but now this can be a much easier task for Mums, Dads, Grandparents, Nannies, Child-minders & Carers of babies.

The NappyTime™ Changing mat now available on Tescos Direct, Amazon & Safetots

This successful British product was invented by Virginia, an ex Rolls-Royce Engineer and a mother of five, when a child she knew was left injured following a fall from a high surface whilst having their nappy changed. The mat will be on sale at the NEC Baby Show, Amazon, Safetots and many retailers across the UK.

The benefits of the NappyTime™ - Changing mat are:

- A rigid board throughout the mat that helps keep your child stable (a 3rd hand)
- A Shoulder/Waist harness that prevents crawling or wriggling away
- A barrier wall that helps prevent fluids reaching babies upper body clothes (less washing)
- A barrier wall that prevents fluids running off the end of the mat onto the surface you are changing them on (i.e. bed, carpet, or adult work clothes)
- A thigh/ankle and kneeling positions on the mat for parent/carer to kneel up or sit astride the mat on the floor for a more ergonomic sitting position, and to prevent back strain from lots of changing nappies
- Can be used up to 36 months

snuggles TIME

PRESS RELEASE!
Wed 5th October 2017

NappyTime™
Changing Mat

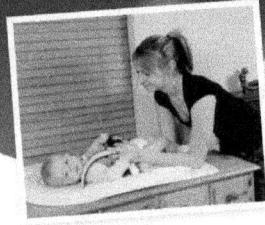

Commenting on the success. NappyTime™ Ltd CEO David Alner said "We can safely say the NappyTime ™ Changing mat is well on its way to being a huge help to many Mums & Dads across the UK. The incredible comments by parents on Amazon are the true view of the people this product set out to and has helped every single day, whilst they need to change nappies. We have NappyTime™ Changing Mats installed in the public facilities of Motorway Services, Shopping Centres, Airports, Selfridges & Legoland Windsor. This mat is available for use at home too.

1. NappyTime™ Limited is a British company based in St. Albans, Hertfordshire.

2. NappyTime™ Changing Mat was designed in the UK and manufactured in the Far East.

3. The consumer profile comprises websites, retailers & public facilities at Motorway Services Airports, Tourist attractions, Shopping Centres, Museums and the Canadian/Australian government.

4. NappyTime™ Limited is also investing in a range of future product developments including: NappyTime™ Newborn, NappyTime™ Changing Unit and NappyTime™ Travel.

5. NappyTime™ Changing Mat was tested to a high standard by BSi's 'General Assessment Procedure', to EN71-3 and BS5852. It was awarded the Platinum Consumer Award at the 'British Invention Show'.

6. During design and development, a range of colours were test marketed and the consumers choice was Classic Cream which is now the core brand product colour.

Need more information? Get in touch...

Mobile
E-mail

Mobile
E-mail

Mobile
E-mail

We're friendly....
Tel 01
E-mail
www.nappy-time.com

And sociable...
Follow us on Twitter
@nappytimemat
Find us on Facebook
Nappytime – Changing Mat

snuggles™ TIME

Blogs

A form of marketing is called a 'Blog'.

Now you can ask your web designer to set you up a section in your website that has a blog page or do this yourself if you are designing the website yourself.

In here you can put all the news you want your current and potential customers to see. Potential customers will review your blog to see what your business has been up to recently, in the past and long term.

Keep it interesting, keep it chipper, keep it upbeat. Best to be positive with a blog as your customers and followers are listening intently.

You can also enlist the services of professional bloggers. They are not too difficult to find. Go to the International Blogging awards website for each country and, if they are any good they will be in the list of award winners. Once you find one on the list, who fits with the type of business you are running, go about politely contacting them.

The Market

(See 'The Business Mountain' - Don't look down (4)
Marketing
You will also find more about the 'Market' in Book 1 -
Startups)

1. For (your business name & business product (s)
    service) ON THE MARKET FROM YEAR ....

Demand will be seen to come from mainly ....

Put here the type of person who will be buying your
product ....

· Firstly - Pregnant people in their third trimester

· Secondly - the over 90's

· Thirdly - Golfers over 25

· Think this over and put the three top person types for
your business.

The Status

Who will recognise the absolute stress-relieving/benefits
of your xyz business?

The products/service of the business will be tremendously
viable and inventive and creative. Customers will feel
comfortable and charmed, exceeding their expectations
as attention to detail is paramount.

The Quality safety and risk assessments, i.e. to the latest ISO certifications/relevant certifications to the utmost and beyond the relevant legal requirements.

Potential customers will have lowest to highest resources and will tend towards those who know what they want.

1. Another of your products
2. Another of your products
3. and so on ..

Demand is seen to come from

.... e.g., the Nursery Industry

.... e.g., the Beauty Industry

..... e.g., the holiday Industry

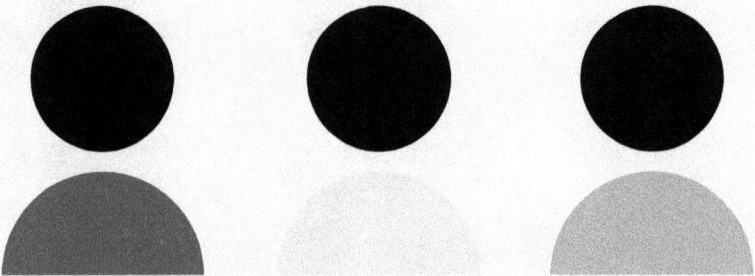

Chapter 12

COMPETITORS

Competition for most businesses comes in many forms. Each presenting different situations for you.

1. Mass producers of similar products

2. Similar service businesses

3. Local competitors

4. National competitors

Competitors may up their advertising and lower their prices to win business.

Many companies' competitors cover their own country only. So, if you are in the USA, many of your competitors will be in the USA too.

Competition can also come from Europe and the World.

For manufactured products, competitors can find ways to circumvent patents. Make sure, with the help of your Patent Attorney that your patent specification minimises the risks of patent infringement.

Patent insurance is another option which may be viable in-order to deter competitive infringers.

Small producers of similar products will need to be monitored.

Foreign manufacturers present the greatness competition. They may produce product in countries not covered by patents. Patenting in all 150/160 civilised countries can prove to be financially prohibitive.

Keep a cursory eye on competitors, make sure they are not infringing any laws that your business must adhere to.

Let us say you have a care home for the elderly in one area, then it will not be possible for a competitor to build a new care home near your one. Check out the legislation/legal requirements for your establishment in the area where you are running your business.

So, you want to open your own barbers' shop in a certain high street. Where do you want your shop? At the end of the high-street away from a very well-established barbers, or right next door or as near as you can get to the very well established business?

Do not ever be afraid of the competition. In this instance, your barbershop is full of customers because you have 'upped your game', your shop front is amazing and inside is stunning ..... When potential customers are walking past both businesses, which one are they going to choose?? Where are they going to go?? You got this my friend, you got this ...

Do not fear your competitors, you can largely ignore them and go outshine them all the way.

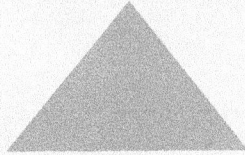

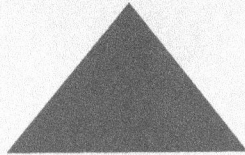

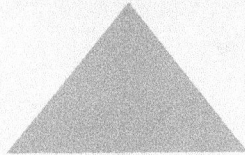

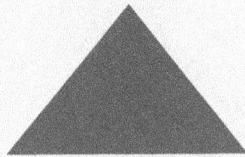

Chapter 13

FUNDING

Capital equipment and materials

Have a long think about what you are going to need.

A computer

A laptop

A desk a chair

An office

A ....

If preparing to manufacture a product list every single component all the types of packaging list everything that incurs a cost however small or large. Everything.

If you are going to launch a patentable product:-

Intellectual property costs

1. Patent attorney fees & Application £
2. Patent search, reporting patent office findings £
3. Patent insurance for patent pending year £
4. Substantive examination fees £
5. Patent office drawings £
6. Patent prosecution costs £
7. Grant certificates £
8. PCT Application costs £

9. Designated Countries £

10. Patent Specifications, Translations £

11. Patent renewal costs £

12. Design registration

.........Your list ?.. go get a pen!!

Component's list/materials list

· Manufacturing Specifications £
· Manufacturing drawings £
· Setting up of Ltd Company £
· Trademarks (your Company name) per Country £
· Trademarks (your product(s) per Country £
· Barcode £
· Barcode registration £

Printing

· Trading standards labels £
· Branding labels
· Customer instructions £
· Product part and serial numbers £
· Operating instructions £
· Customer registration card (check legislation mandatory for USA/Canada/Australia £
· Leaflets £
· Posters £
· Purchase Order forms £
· Invoices £

- Handout cards £
- Exhibition's competition cards £
- Business Cards £
- Compliment's aments slip £
- Headed A4 paper £
- Packaging (pvc or cardboard box)£
- 4-or 2 or 1 Colour cartons £

Marketing/Publicity £ (Could be up to 20% of turnover)

Training (Could be 15% of turnover)

Newspaper/magazine copy £

NappyTime™
Changing Mat

Nappy Time Limited
Unit 203, Second Floor
China House
401 Edgware Road
London NW2 6GY
VAT Reg No. 177 8249 59

Customer Invoice No.

NT

Purchase Order No.

Date

/ /2015

UK ORDER FORM

PLEASE USE BLOCK CAPITALS

Invoice Details

Company		Contact	
Address		Position	
		Mob	
City		Tel	
County		Fax	
Postcode		E-mail	
Country		Web	

Delivery Details

(Please block if same
as invoice details)

Site Name	
Address	
City	
County	
Postcode	
Tel	
Special Instructions	

Product Details

| Description | NappyTime™ Changing Mat 380mm x 760mm QTY 1 | Min. Order Quantity | 1 Mat |

Order Details

Description	Pallet Size (mm)	Mats	Quantity	Trade Price Per Mat	RRP	Units	Price Per Unit	Total
	600 x ...	1		£12.99				£
	900 x 373 x 750	9		£11.99				
	1200 x 1000 x 900	81		£10.99				
	1200 x 1000 x 1550	162		£10.99				
Basic Fixing Kit G ***				£15.00	£25.00			
							Sub total	£
							Shipping & Packaging	£
							Fuel surcharge	
							VAT	£
All prices, costs and payments are specified in GBP sterling							TOTAL	£

*** Includes: 2 x Fixing Plates, 6 x Screws, 6 x Screw Caps, 2 x A3 Laminated Safety Posters, 50cm Sticky Fixer Tape, 1 x A4 Instruction Sheet, 1 PVC Bag.
Please note: ALL mat purchases for use in public baby changing rooms require a fixing kit.

Payment Details

NappyTime ™ Ltd

Cheques payable to:

NappyTime ™ Ltd
287 High Street
London Colney
St.Albans AL2 1EU

Tel 01727 822779
E-mail sales@nappy-time.com

www.nappy-time.com

snuggles

Payments Accepted:
Cheque, Bank Transfer.

Refunds & Exchanges
Baby hygiene products cannot be resold if returned for reasons of hygiene. It is at the discretion of the Company wether or not the customer is entitled to a full refund upon return of goods.

NappyTime ™ Ltd. Registered in England. Company Reg No 7790661. Patented & Designed in the UK Patent No GB2357965

Country populations (check for changes)

Italy 60m

Spain 46m

Japan 126m

France 67m

Germany 83m

United Kingdom 67 million

Australia 25m

Canada 37m

United States of America 328m

China 1.398Bn

Russia 144m

Denmark 5.8m

Sweden 10.2m

Hong Kong 7.5M

(Many more countries could be designated but sufficient funding to cover in further Countries will be needed)

If you are patenting in Countries across the world, there are many you can patent in, 126 Countries last time I counted. Have a think about which Countries have the manufacturing skills and the ability to copy your product(s) they are the ones to cover (this can be expensive). I also cover Hong Kong as it is still the gateway to China and often goods still come through Hong Kong to depart China, so it makes sense to Patent in Hong Kong too.

Materials required to start up production

I will now set out the materials that I require to set up for production of one of my own products for you ...

PVC SHEETING

FOAM

PVC/HARDBOARD/CARDBOARD

TOWELLING

DISPOSABLE CLOTHS

HANGER BAG

PRINTING

WEBBING

BUCKLES

The current value to the business of this product and existing agreements is £xx.yy

(See annual account published at Companies House .... on this date xx/yy/zzzz)

————- Now go make your own list ————

What will you need…? for a bed and breakfast

PROPERTY £

BEDS £

MATTRESSES £

SHEETS (white only) £

TABLES £

CUTLERY £

CROCKERY £

FRIDGE £

FREEZER £

WATER HEATER £

TOWELS (white only) £

…. etc ….

———- Enjoy doing this list for yourself ———-

Get is right check it with your advocates and your accountant, <u>mistakes can be costly</u>.

INSURANCE COSTS

Intellectual property Patent Insurance £

Public liability £

Personal liability £

Professional liability £

Product liability £

Product re-call £

Motor fleet £

Stop loss £

Keyman/Key woman insurance £

—— Now go make your insurance list ——

You can create your insurance list yourself or with the help of an insurance broker.

Working capital for the launch of product(s)/ service

The need for working capital can be restrained in two ways…

1. Not being pressurised by outside sources/advice to do all the groundwork too quickly.

2. Only launch business once the following have been created. If you are prepared you can forecast and prepare for the likely costs.

Business Plan

Marketing Plan

Manufacturing Specifications & Drawings

Draft licence agreement

Costed Technical program

Approved Suppliers listing

Patent Specification

List of potential manufacturers

Working capital for upholding patent/fees

Proprietor own personal funds will sustain the business until the (your product(s)/service) is brought to market.

Sources of finance will be found for

X costs

Y costs

Z costs

Etc ....

By xx/yy/zzzz date

A licence will be granted by *yourself* to (your Company) to commercialise your product(s)/service. See The Business Mountain - Don't look down book (x) for licence information or contact your business Lawyer to create a licence for yourself and your business.

It is my preference, but I file all patents and trademarks and design registrations in my own name and then I licence them out personally to the Companies commercialising the products/business including my own businesses that I work for/in.

This will protect your personal finances from the activities of your businesses if the correct clauses are put into the licence.

This is to account for all initial payments and pre-payments for all mandatory Safety certifications for the business (Your company) patent fees trademark fees and any other starting up a business cost.

Patent Attorney agents will safeguard on-time payments for the business into the future.

Typical funding arrangements

Finance of £....... will be sought to fund the setting up of the medium sized business to develop the (expansion of the franchise) (the setting up of (x) more shops). Moving the start-up to small business to a medium sized business. Funds will need to be available from day one launch day.

Once launch date has passed all staff will be contracted and salaried.

Personal cash requirements

When you are preparing to launch your own business, you must factor in your personal costs/wages for yourself, so they are all covered as you prepare for launch.

Founders needs for wages are often overlooked and sacrificed at launch time but they **must** be addressed.

Try to save up your cash reserves ready to sustain yourself and your family dependents for your pre-launch period.

Talk to your accountant in this respect too. If you are planning to be VAT registered, then your pre-launch business purchase receipts may be eligible for VAT refunds. If your start-up costs are high let us say you are opening a hotel and your start-up purchase receipts add up to a lot of money. You will be pleased to receive back a VAT refund on your purchases.

Check with your accountant how long before your launch date you can apply for a VAT refund for. Laws change regularly so therefore you should check with a qualified accountant what the laws are for your financing.

—————— Save and learn and launch ——————-

SEE APPENDICES FOR OPERATING PROFITABILITY AND CASH FLOW PROJECTIONS

As in the typical finance forms set out in chapter 3 it is good to have all of these set out and (filled out with **'your real figures'** at the back of your business plan amongst all of your appendices).

You will also find sample Excel spreadsheets for business financing including profit/loss turnover and breakeven points for you in Virginia's websites and The Business Mountain APP

www.rabbitts.com

www.thebusinessmountain.com

Chapter 14

WITHIN PLAIN SIGHT

Business Reporting

Monitoring of all (Your business name) statistics for the following:

1. Word of mouth

2. Enquiries by customers

3. Quotations for customers

4. Conversion rate for customers

5. Orders for customers

6. Sales via website

7. Sales via APP

8. Sales at exhibitions

9. Sales via 'Social Media' adverts

10. Sales via business video

11. Sales via competitions

12. Etc …

Now go get a pen & do your list !!

All by number and value monthly

(Your Business name) will assess trends and time lags between each.

It is important that we monitor where our sales are coming from and how many sales are coming from each specific sales avenue.

Once we can see the pattern for this forming, we can tailor our business to where the business is at.

Monitoring

It will be necessary for (Your business name) to monitor production and productivity as well as financial results and progress.

Weekly costings

The (Your business name) Finance department will provide weekly costings sheets for (Your business name) to complete and return to show the hours utilised each day. This will combine with the need for productivity costings. There will be one sheet for each sheet designated.

Costing information will be transferred to a computer to record the costing permanently:

· Per product and overall, per batch

· Of all part numbers and batch numbers and dates produced

If let us say you have a hotel, for your purchase orders you can give all the products you need your own Company's individual part numbers.

So, towels would be (Your company's first 4 letters|date|your number)

There are inventory software systems you can either have tailored to your own business or that you can buy off the shelf for your business.

These will tell you how much stock you have onsite how much you will need into the future and will flag up for you when you are running low on individual items.

With this you will need to take into account wastage so will need to have regular wastage checks too.

- All finance records to conform to the requirements of 'Trading Standards' for traceability of all transactions. (It is much better to ensure that your business conforms to Trading standards rules so if you ever have to involve Trading Standards in your business you already meet their requirements.

- With all details recorded for the current period and accumulatively.

- Make a link with your quotations and to standard times for work to access productivity. This will include individual task costings that have standard costs.

Performance measures

Will test and monitor your business's performance

Profit & Loss

Monthly profit and loss accounts will be produced by (Your business name) and a 'Balance Sheet' and Cashflow too will be produced monthly.

(These figures will give you insights into how your business is doing/progressing. So, you can make adjustments if you realise you need to from the results each month that you get to look over).

Chapter 15

TRAINING

Training

Business training courses for proprietor provided by:-

· Your own Local business training centre (name)

· Online training providers (x/y&z)

· Chambers of Commerce (Your County)

· A training program will be set up immediately for all (Your business name) staff

· XYZ associates and mentors will provide guidance at launch and start-up

All accounting procedures will be made clear to proprietor by Chartered Accountant (name)

All patenting queried will be made clear by

· The Patent Office

· Patent Attorney (state name)

· Mentors from (your mentors)

· Appointed Solicitors (Your Solicitors named)

The Business Mountain books, and the internet will be researched for all aspects and information required for running the business of (Your business name)

The Business Mountain books, and the internet will be researched for all aspects and information required for running the business of (Your business name)

YOUR LOCAL BUSINESS TRAINING CENTRE

SHOULD PROVIDE YOU WITH LOW-COST TRAINING SESSIONS WHICH WILL HELP YOU TO LEARN HOW TO RUN YOUR OWN BUSINESS

THE TYPES OF COURSES YOU ARE LOOKING FOR WILL BE :-

Business planning workshop

Presentation skills workshop

Sales tips for small businesses

GDPR and Data protection seminar

E-Mail marketing

Time management seminar

Grievance handling & motivation

Coaching & counselling

Bookkeeping seminar

Introduction to social media

Pricing for profitability

Facebook & Instagram for business

Building a successful brand seminar

Business planning (There may be more than one of these business planning workshops)

Search engine optimisation workshop

Google analytics workshop

Setting up an online business seminar

Business plan into action workshop

'The Business Mountain' will be launching a range of on-line courses for you ASAP

For staff training make sure they all have their basic training

GDPR and Data protection training

Health & Safety training

First Aid training

Language's training

Relevant to your business training

IT security

A)

B)

C)

D)

E)

It is customary for the corporate businesses to spend around the 15% mark of profits on training. This way you are investing in your business by investing in your staff. This is shown as a guide and is not compulsory. Look at your current and projected finances with your accountant for each year.

On-line there are now countless companies doing training packages.

Some are watch a video then take an exam others are log in to see your tutor with other people being trained at the same time. Choose your training packages carefully.

Chapter 16

SALES/PRODUCTION/
PRODUCTIVITY

Sales/Production/Productivity

Initially sales are likely to directly relate to the response from the advertising campaign launch placed in x/y/z magazines and the website pre-launch and the website formal launch. Editorial copy can be commissioned in all relevant magazines and news papers. Press, social media, news releases and special photographs can be prepared in advance.

Transcripts can be run through one or more AI app's for suggestions beyond own advertising slogans/paragraphs/sentences & statements or a professional Copywriter can be hired to produce the correct words for sales pitches.

When advertising via social media I.e with an Ads campaign this will test your ads assets like your video'/reel/stories and copyrighting.

Look out for your 'Quality' ranking, your engagement rate ranking, conversion ranking. If these metrics are all good the less money you will spend and the more likely your campaign will be successful.

This is where it becomes exciting for us ...we put in all the hard work and our efforts start to bear fruit. Just like a tree, waiting for it to grow, from a seed to a seedling then waiting for it to bear fruit.

As you make all these efforts to bring in the sales. Make sure you measure each one. Then you will be able to tell if they are effective or not and if they were worth the investment. What is the sales value minus the marketing investment? Your accountant may be able to help you analyse this data specific to your business.

Here I have a sales measuring form for you to use yourself. It is also known as a **'Guard Book'**

FOR EACH COMPETITION/ ADVERTISEMENT/ OR INSET/BANNER etc...	
DATE INSERT APPEARED	
TITLE MAGAZINE/SM/NEWSPAPER	
Page Data Appeared	
Circulation of News Paper/Magazine/SM	
RESPONSE - SALES	
Number of Sales '000	
Total Sales $/£/€/¥	
RESPONSE (%)	
No. of Requests + Number of Salea	
COSTS	
Media Cost	
Leaflet Cost (Including costs of mailing)	
TOTAL COST	
COST EFFECTIVENESS	
Total Sales ($/£/€/¥)	
Average Order Value Sales + No. of Orders	
COST PER ORDER (Total costs above + No of Orders)	
Sales $/£/€/¥ per thousand pounds/ dollars/Euros/Yuen Spent	

The Business you've started is a fish & chip shop in the heart of your own town. You decide to start off with a social media video to alert your potential customers and bring in initial sales. You organise a targeted social media campaign which determines the age group| where they shop|what their likes are etc etc then you launch the ad for a designated period of time and a designated amount of spend.

See what happens ... this is like like Pandora's box, no one knows what will happen to each of your sales generating efforts. Other fish & chip shops are unlikely to think of using social media to ... do this but this is the way of the future. The social media giants know that the local business es are missing a trick as we say here ... but we know too now.

(Your Company name) Products will be sold via mail order/ over the counter/purchase orders/pre-orders/web or app online forms.

For patent pending products sales will be made of manufactured products during the patent pending year WITH AN INITIAL TEST MARKET OF SAY 250 units.

If necessary adverts will be put into all the trade magazines too that are given out free to your target audience e.g. pregnant people or the elderly (whichever relevant)

Anyone wishing to sign up our monthly wishing to sign up to our monthly newsletter by inputting their contact details will be directed to our presence in another company's mailing app, so all GDPR laws are abided by. In this instance a mailing App like 'Mail-Chimp' would be used.

Sales for instance for a product will be made eventually to:

1. The Sheds
2. The high street retailers
3. Supermarkets
4. Shopping tv channels
5. Independent retailers
6. Wholesalers

For say a restaurant:

1. Families
2. Elderly
3. Couples
4. Workers
5. Clubs
6. Celebrations

Now go do your list for your type of business:

1. X
2. Y
3. Z
4. A
5. B
6. C
7. D

Ensuring sales by (Your business name) in designated Countries by (Your business name)

Just so you know for future time-based calculations:-

Note standard annual hours for individuals 1800 hours per annum.

16.1 Production targets - First Year

The manufacturer will have to designate hours available for production. Each product will be made within x-hours for the first year.

16.2 Production targets - Second Year

When you start up your business the timings will be set for a period of time. Once up and running you can look to reduce working times (Also known as 'Working Time Directive')

Building up to production at the rate of each product made in half of one hour.

16.3 It remains to be tested whether it will be possible to meet the above production targets. Bearing in mind there will be wasted time in manufacturing as new product and concept, and some development may occur during production schedules.

There will also be some time spent by (Your Company name) which will be non-chargeable:-

- **Negotiating with manufacturers**
- **Advisors**
- **Negotiating with suppliers**
- **Marketing & promotion**

Non- productive time would be between 10% - 20% of available time to (Your Business name)

You may find your non-productive time in your working week may need to be monitored by you. Negotiating with suppliers, making phone calls, reading e-mails all take time. This is where time management comes in.

Try to structure your day so you get the most out of the time you have to be productive.

You can pre-plan your days out some of the time ...

Emails are a great time waster. You can set yourself a time of day to read through them all initially and try to do the replies as you read them. Or leave the replies until you have all the information you require to reply within relevant timescales.

Now go do your todo list ....

- ....
- ....
- ....

Product pricing

A system for product/service use pricing

Standard systems be in place to provide a set of standard prices; these will be, computer program based and will be highly automated. Each sales type will be listed (in for example Excel) then analysed.

Standards will be set based on a fast and efficient manufacturing operation, and these will form the basis of all costs for the sale prices for the different derivatives of the products.

The working time for production of products can change with time and can be analysed.

It is anticipated that these standards will not be reached in early months of the first year through the second year should see significant improvements.

Targets and goals can be set. If not met they can be measured and adjusted according to own business standards.

The cost of making the product will take account of the entire system and handwork or robot or machine work and will be related to work units of measurement, which will ensure that the derivative is recognised and is directly related to costings.

Packaging costs and delivery costs must be addressed and and included within the budget.

Allocate each of the standard product range items a part-number and a serial number too when appropriate which will be linked to date of sale and a customer invoice. (Then if you ever have to do a recall of product the numbers will direct you to the correct batch records of products made)

Now your prices

You need to label your products with the prices your customers are willing to pay (See 'The Business Mountain - Don't look down - Book 1 STARTUPS' Really you are working backwards from this expected price.

Let's look at an example:-

So, you are selling long dresses on-line and in Department stores they cost £20 in materials and dressmaking costs. Your customers love your brand for which you have your own recognised and familiar 'logo' so your customers are prepared to pay £650 per dress. Now your costs can be low, so you have a high profit to manufacture ratio.

As your customers are prepared to pay this much for your specific design of a dress, your packaging and labels and materials must also be of good quality as there is an expectation that will derive from your customers that is what they are expecting of your brand.

Branded tissue paper ... your own logo blended into the lining of a garment. All the building blocks of trust in your brand.

A System for Product Pricing

By Law you cannot 'fix' your final selling price to the customer. You can only recommend your product is sold for a certain price.

In the service industry in the main your customers will be your direct customers paying the price that you have given them.

For products that can be sold to third party sales outfits you can only recommend the price that you believe that your product should be sold for. And discounts that third parties introduce to their customers you can negotiate/discuss and agree upon.

Chapter 17

PREMISES

Premises

Premises for your business need to be carefully thought out.

If you want to open a restaurant make sure there is enough of a footprint (square meterage of floorspace) on the premises you have chosen for (and working backwards again) the daily turnover you need to achieve.

So, you work out how many tables you will need in your restaurant to achieve your planned turnover. Tables achieve covers so you can work out how many covers you can achieve for lunchtime and how many covers are your target for suppertime.

An example of the target for lunchtime is 120 covers. These are 'bums on seats' ... to put it crudely. So, the maximum number of people you can accommodate over one sitting at 120 seats per session starting at 12pm and finishing at 2.30pm. Sometimes you can turn a table around again and get two sets of covers off one table. This is a bonus for your business, but cannot be relied upon.

Be realistic and plan what is possible for your business.

This is pure maths & will let you know the maximum turnover your Business can achieve.

If the figures don't add up then maybe you need a larger or a smaller premises for your restaurant.

Until the end of the year xx/yy/zzzz

The Business is planned to occupy premises for the starting up (working from home) at the address already given.

The use of other premises is unlikely to be of benefit.

From xx/yy/zzzz

The business will occupy a headquarters of 100 sq.ft/ 10 sq. meters (12 members of staff) in an open plan office setting. Adjust accordingly.

You will need to consider the space your staff need to work in and there is a **certain amount of floor space you will need for each member of your staff.**

Our office(s) in .... may require ...... sq.ft.//meters.

Listen carefully.... Many Ltd Companies have their accountant's business address as their business address. So, their business is registered at their accountant's address.

This can be for many reasons, so you will carefully need to consider your reasons and the address you want to use for your business.

You can still use your business premises address for all suppliers and other business contacts who are likely to send you post but HMRC, Companies house & all formal mailings will go to your "Registered Address".

When taking over any form of contract or lease over a building that you will use for business purposes, please read all the small print and don't get caught for £200,000 worth of renovations of a building. I came across a business that didn't read the small print and didn't realise that they were responsible for imminent building renovations that it would take their profits away for years (for on a building they would only end up with less lease time on it) BE CAREFUL!!

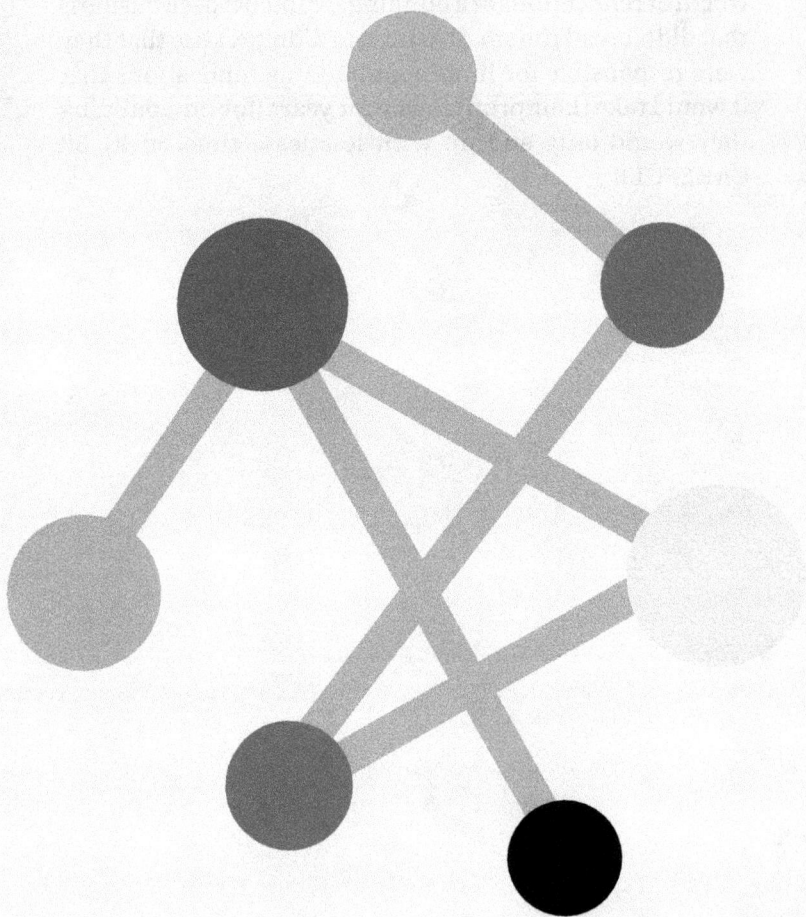

Chapter 18

MANAGEMENT SYSTEMS

Management Systems

(Your Business name) will put in the following systems to monitor performance and this may form the base for the improvement of the operating of the business.

Accounting

Systems will provide the necessary bookkeeping function but will also provide information on costs and income. This will be provided on the monthly, quarterly, and annual basis via an accounting software package.

Contracts

A contract record will be maintained for every enquiry. This will give details of the contract and of the work-related enquiry. If the contract proceeds to retailer the record will linkup and show the stages of progression.

There will be an evaluation/report on each contract and for each contact person with that organisation. For each organisation there will be many contacts each with their own individual record with date and serial number.

Records/Risk assessments and filing and archiving should all be organised and managed.

Contact/Transaction

These will be recorded and linked to the contact record.

Information on Company Sales Contact Record

Contact number :-

Date;-

Name of person contacted:-

Organisation of person contacted:-

Phone number of person contacted

Retailer order placed:-

CRM systems: Customer Relationship Management' Systems are available via Apps/Websites

It is best to look into these systems to find out what is the best system for your business. You may not need one of these software based systems but it is up to you.

These systems help to manage customer data and sales data and can be integrated with your social media platform pages.

Retailer code 1:-

Retailer code 2:-

Retailer code 3:-

Retailer code 4:-

Number & nature of products ordered (product code):-

Price quoted:-

Delivery dates quoted:-

Hourly rate applicable from manufacturer:-

Standard manufacturing time (hours & value)

Price charged:-

Date agreement settled:-

Memorandum note for:

1. Problems with manufacture

2. Measurement of customer satisfaction

3. Problems with retailer - before & after delivery

4. Problems with customers - before & after delivery

Statistics

It is best to compile information by Month, Quarter and Year.

This will include the following for service and manufacturing businesses.

·   No of products ordered for different outlets

·   Conversion rate

·   Elapsed time - Enquiry to order

·   Value of order - Hour's value

·   STANDARD TIME

·   Time utilisation - Productive time

·   Productive standard hours

·   Non-productive hours

·   Time spent

·   Materials costs including VAT.

·   Finishing value

·   Materials on cost

·   Sales value

All the above are fairly all encompassing for all businesses. If you know of anymore that need to be on your list pls add them. All this information paints a picture of how your business is doing, growing, not growing, struggling.

If your business is flourishing and your accountant can confirm this. Keep going. IF your business isn't flourishing/growing start to evaluate what is happening in your business. If the business model you have cannot be made to work then consider a change of direction within your business. Or a major or a complete change of direction. Or exit and choose a new business idea.

Chapter 19

RISKS

High

Product recall costs.

Manufacturer has difficulties keeping up with demand.

Contracts which have leaks with manufacturers/ suppliers/retailers/wholesalers/volume sellers.

Patents awarded for products are possible. It is possible to enlist the support of a Patent Attorney to aid a successful patent application.

Copyright of business data not protected.

Trademarks not registered with your Government Intellectual property office.

Staf spoiling your business. Without your knowledge you can find that your wealth jealous staff are divesting your business of your staff or your customers. Watch out for this, as all your staff may need to do to affect this is to be rude to your other members of staff or be incredibly rude to your own customers, or even your potential interested customers.

Staff may have decided for you that you are rich enough and they will slow your custom. They can do this over a period of 20+ years without you noticing. To devastate your business. Bad Management Staff have been known to divest businesses of up to 65% of on-site staff. If your staff turnover goes over 5% per annum get your grievance handling Human Resources expert in to address the damage to your business and to rectify staff shortages.

- Excessive non-productive time in manufacture

- Legal costs for policing of patents inside the U.K.

- Legal costs for policing of patents outside the U.K.

- Urgent need to export as the export side of a business can be a large percentage of business success.

- Product defects

Bad publicity or marketing errors should be watched out for. These need to be retracted or overcome as swiftly as possible IMMEDIATELY.

You can hire a publicly agency to keep negative publicity from damaging your business as swiftly as possible.

Unforeseen circumstances and World-wide/ country wide disasters can be a high-risk threat to your business.

One main way to prepare for this type of risk is to create for your business a 'War Chest' . A financial buffer, in terms of cash or/and property to do your best to be prepared for future unforeseen disasters which can then have more of a chance to be survived by your business.

Tsunamis, flooding. Foot & Mouth, Mad cow disease, Covid to name but a few of past problematic disasters which affected some but not all businesses terribly.

Medium

Proprietor health

Major retailers dragging their heels.

- Lack of interest in product, no sales

- Excessive time taken in production in early years
- Advertising & Marketing overspend
- Publicity errors
- Price too high for too long

Low

Poor quality of production under pressure.

Some of these you will know are the same for you and your business ... now go list your risks to your business in the categories of high, medium and low. Try to think of everything you possibly can. Business interruption is the worst one to me. Is there anything that would completely interrupt your business for a sustained period? Like 'Foot & Mouth' in 2001 decimated the horse racing and the bookmakers' businesses.

Then mad cow disease or BSE disease 1996 did the same to the same industries a few years later.

The Covid situation for business has been a business interrupter and a business closer. If you understand these tricky times can be experienced by any business, then you can factor in your response and your preparations in the event of interruptions.

Chapter 20

ACTION PLAN

Action plan

An essential element of the setting up is to undertake the writing of this plan. This will map out the prospective course of the business and will deal with current aspects of the business and of those of the future.

Following the agreement of this plan the steps outlined will be implemented.

It will be necessary to consider each step in the sequence of events to ensure a structured approach for the development of the business.

The critical path will be analysed.

The full action plan will be produced by (Your Company Name) as a separate document by the Managing Director and senior staff and/or Director/Board members.

This will be your plan completed. Now we turn to your Appendices.

Appendices

A Resource Analysis

(Your Business name) Resource Analysis Assessments

A.1 Objectives:-

- To establish a new (xyz type business) creating (xyz) products for a Worldwide market .... / ..... Creating a local village/shop business for the local people .... / ..... Creating a new online business for our Country/ the World.

- To expand the business so it is a)self-sustaining shop in the local village)/(so products are sold Worldwide over the period of 20 years of the Patent)

- With a solid business foundation that will allow further business expansion into the future.

- Protecting the business from infringement and copiers where legally possible.

- To attempt to keep most of the employment in own country.

A.2 Expenditure Plan :-

Cash needed pre-launch in (wxyz year ... I.e., 2078)

Capital Revenue

Insurances:- £.....................

Electrical Equipment:- £.......................

(I.e., computer/laptop/printer/mobile phone(s)

Other Capital Equipment:- £...........................

(Business specific)

Patent Costs:- £.......................

Cash needed for (wxyz - following year ... I.e., 2079)

Xyz units manufactured

Capital Equipment

I.e., for a B&B all bathrooms and bedrooms

Other costs :- £........................

Total capital equipment required for year 1 £.........

(Including Pre-Launch)

Total cash needed for year 1 £.........

For (Your Company name)

An xyz Company providing abc products/service....

Include:- Company setup costs/Marketing costs Exhibition costs/Advertising costs/

Public Relations costs

Total capital equipment required for year 2 £............

Total cash needed for year 2 £.................

for (Your Company name)

List costs

1. a
2. b
3. c
4. d
5.

Appendices B.1

(You're Company Name) Income Plan

Cash needed in 2027 as sample:-

Project Commitment Tooling Costs
£x,yyy

Trademark/Patent/Copyright Costs
£x,yyy

Manufacturing Costs
£x,yyy

Insurance Costs
£x,yyy

Overheads Costs
£x,yyy

Royalty Costs (% Of T.o.)
£x,yyy

Public Relations Costs
£x,yyy

Marketing Costs
£x,yyy

Advertising Costs
£x,yyy

Continue this list with all your business costs.....

Appendix C

Employee Data

C.1 (A)

Single Person Full Time Employment

Annual data - Productive days:-

Standard. 45 weeks

5 days a week

Total standard hours 1,800 hours per year

Possible additional, say: 34 weeks

1 day per week

6 hours per day

Total additional premium hours say 200 hrs per employee (overtime)

Total maximum hours   2000 hrs per annum per employee

C.1 (B) Single Person Part-Time Employment

45 weeks

5 days per week

5 hours per day

Total Standard hours 1,125

Appendix D

Here is an example for you of a product range with its part number list:-

For you it may be better for you to keep all of this for your products private.

This below is to provide you with an amazing example of how all this pre-planning works.

This was written many years ago, but it may all provide you with an in insight into how to analyse your potential minimum and maximum potential sales......

Product Range : Kelly's Kettles™

	Part Numbers. Rrp	
• 'Classic Kellykettle™'	£24=95	KKPO001
• 'Classic Kellytoaster'	£29=95	KKPO002
• 'Classic KellyJucier'	£74=95	KKPO003
• 'Classic Kellyhandwisk'	£12=95	KKPO0004
• 'Classic Kellyminiwhisk'	£3=45	KKPO0005
• 'Classic Kellycutlery'	£14=95	KKPO0006
• 'Classic Kellytoastie'	£19.99	KKPO0007

Note:-

Leave room for your part-numbers by putting in sufficient zeros. This leaves space for the products you will be selling into the future.

Use a recognisable start to your part-numbers. Here they have been started with simply 'KK' these are the initials for the Example Business 'Kellykettles' ... now go and construct the basis for your part numbers for all of your current and future products.

Predicted Sales in the U.K.

To give just an idea of 1% of sales potential in one country for a single product see below:-

Note: The British National Statistics for the number of households in the U.K. per annum. (CHECK THIS, IT CHANGES EVERY YEAR)

Example A: Absolute Minimum Sales (United Kingdom only) - assumes 1% of 28.1mn Households generates sales

£29.95 x 281,000 units (1% households in United Kingdom in any one year)

= £8,415,950

Example B: Minimum assuming at least 2 products bought per household

£29.99 x 281,000 units x 2 (1% of households x2 in England & Wales pa)

= £16,831,900 inc Vat

Example C: Assuming at least 4 products bought per household

£29.95 x 281,000 x4 units (**1%** of 28,100,000 for U.K. pa over 4 years) = £33,663,800

(None Of The Above Calculations Include Sales Of The Other Accessories)

·······················oooOOOOooo·····························

Theoretical Maximum Sales Per Annum

Example D: Maximum Sales assuming Sales in United Kingdom only

£29.95 x 28,100,000 x 0.25 (25% of U.K. households per annum) = £210,398,750

All the above examples are for example unit sales only with no account for sales of the full range of products.

You will hear Companies boast they have up to 57% of their market share. This is not a given but can happen. It is said that 1% is guaranteed & takes minimal marketing.

'Unique Accessories And Matching Products'

Target market = 28.1mn households

i.e. there will be at any one time:-

Uk Sales In The Second Year

E.g. : Kellykettles ™

Sales in the second year, will depend upon sales in the first, and will depend upon the correct messages about the product going out to the public about all the new benefits on offer with the new system, and having the product available for the public to purchase when they want to, and not waiting for it to be available.

The sales growth chart will indicate sales potential given the ratios of the curve and the speed at which the sales line is ascending towards its plateau level this in turn will allow us to calculate the number of employees to recruit the workspace required etc....and the probability of sales values.

The sales predictions above cover the UK only but as there are (?) Billion households worldwide throughout the World every year the world target market is on a much wider scale and could be tackled in due course.

Export Sales In Third Year

TBA by Appointed Managing Director

Appendix E

Finance and Overview

The forecast financial activities are given for a four-year period.

(A) The First Company operation option: Instruct Designated Manufacturers/choose suppliers for your B&B/Hotel/Coffee shop

To manufacture the first product only and deliver it to (Your Company name) headquarters which will subsequently package products individually and deliver to the Retailers/Wholesalers.

(Your Company) will control patents as above and promote market the product in house.

(B) The Second Company option: Sell licences for distributorships to Trade Organisations

To distribute the product within defined borders in specific countries

The Schedules Are As Follows:-

E.1.1 Expenses.

E1.2 Sales and Net Profit / -Loss figures for four years.

E.1.3 Break-even analysis.

E.1.4 Standard Production hours.
Value of products made.

E.1.5 Quarterly Business incremental build-up.

E.1.6 Summary of productive hours; (with lost hours evaluation)

E.1.7 Average value per unit(s) sold

E.2 Monthly profit and loss Account

E.3 Monthly cashflow

E.4 Balance Sheet

Appendix F   DATE : xx/yy/zzzz

(Your Business Name)

Overheads And Profitabiliy

F 1 Profitability Summary

An example of a kettle manufacturer

Note

(a) There are at least 28.1 million households in the U.K.(Check by using a Search Engine No. of households in your Country and the year that you are living in)

(b) All following calculations are based upon one unit kettle sale price £29=95 inc Vat.

(c) The product does have the potential of matching products sales i.e., toasters of different sizes & juicers all in matching colourways for its extended range.

YEAR 1 SALES (MINIMUM) Launch to Test Market single standard Kellykettle™

Potential Sales   £281,000 (11,224 Units pa)

Costs

Cost to Manufacture   £67,231(¼ of 281,000 generally)

(This should include your business premises/running costs and cost of materials & tooling for manufacture ... Don't forget tooling costs !!)

Be careful here. Talk to your Accountant to get it right.

Hours to Manufacture in UK   4826 hours
(Based upon 1 unit Manu in 43 minutes..... check this)

Staff required   3 members of staff

Labour costs (£13 pphr including NI contributions) £ 62,738 (4826 x 3 people x £13 =£ 62,738)

Capital Investment required to cover Manufacturing & materials   £130,000 (67,231+£62,738)

As a benchmark many companies use a portion of their profits as follows

Marketing (25% of profits ... you decide) & Training (15% of profits.... You decide)

This is called investing in your business.

Over heads   £67,231

Royalties(to include patents around 7% of Manu costs) £4706 (7% pf £67,231)

Royalty percentages can be anything from 1% to around 7% of the trade price dependent upon T.O. and negotiation skills. A licencing practitioner can help you with Royalty fees negotiations.

==========

Turnover   £281,000

==========

Profit   £146,325 (£281,000 - £67,231)

==========

Year 2 Sales   (Minimum)

Potential Sales   £xxxxxxx

• aaaa units CP=£yy.yy RRP=£zz.zz

RRP=£bb.bb

Costs

Cost to manufacture   £yy.yy

Capital Investment   £ccccccc

Marketing & Manufacturing

Overheads   £xxxxxxx
Salaries   £xxxxxxx
Royalties   £xxxxxxx

(Always!! put in an amount for salaries, you may be planning to set it all up in your spare time, remember no one works for free in a Business and you will need to quantify the salary amounts

to build them into your financial forecasting for the future.)

==========

£ yyyyyyyyyy

==========

Profit

£ zzzzzzzzz

==========

Units To Be Sold   xxxxxxx ===>   yyyyyyyyy Hours Work

Number Of Employees : xxx employees

To break even we would need to sell :-   ? units

This is without considering the following **additional vast potential sales:-**

• Potential sales of xyz product accessories

• Potential sales xyz exports

• All the other products in range

F 2 Profitability Summary Calulations

Potential Business to Cover (Your Company) Costs

	Share Of The
Total Costs	Market For Uk Only

-- =

Households in UK x Sale Price Of Unit

£

-- =

E.g., 28.1mn   x   £yyyyy

F 3

To cover Manufacturing Costs

For 100,000 Products Sold

100,000 Units x £yyyyyy each product

(Number of products sold x price of product £yyyyy = yyyyyyyyy

	AA% of xxxxxxxxx	=
Profit	BB% of yyyyyyyyy	=

Hence for a manufacturer they would need

$$\frac{100,000}{28,100,000} = 0.138 = 0.35\% \text{ of U.K.}$$

of the market share in the U.K. to break even.

(Your Company) Start Up Costs

This is without considering the following *additional potential sales:-*

- Potential sales of xyz product accessories
- Potential sales xyz exports
- All other products in range

F 4 Profitability Summary

Current

Year....................

£ ....Sales   £ ....

£ ....Less Purchases   £ ....

£ ....Carriage   £ ....

£ ....Packing
materials   £ ....

£ ....   £ ....

£ ....Net Operating
Income (loss?)   £ ....

Administrative Expenses

Year................

£	Insurance	£ ....
£	Post and Stationery	£ ....
£	Telephones	£ ....
£	Broadband	£ ....
£	Sundry Expense	£ ....
£	Advertising/Marketing	£ ....
£	Training	£ ....
£	Motor expenses	£ ....
£	Entertaining, Travel, Hotels & Subsistence	£ ....
£	Repairs & Renewals	£ ....
£	Legal & Professional Fees	£ ....
£	Bank charges	£ ....
£	Depreciation	£ ....
£	Bad Debts	£ ....
£	Total Expenses	£ ....
£	Net Loss	£ ....

Assets

£yyyyyyyy enterprise grants

£yyyyy other grants

£yyyyyy Loan

£yyyyyy Bank Business Current Account

£yyyyy Bank Business Savings Account

£yyyyyyy Sales

================================

£yyyyyyy Total

£yyyyyy to find   option of extra £yyyyy LOAN

0.1 Patent Status

Patent Costs:-

Minimum PCT/European Worldwide Patent Costs Forecast: -Date____European Patent: Due by xx/yy/zz

£yyyyyy will include (List Countries)Date____ USA: Due by xx/yy/zz £yyyyyDate____Japan: Due by xx/yy/zz £yyyyyyDate____Australia: Due by xx/yy/zz £yyyyyyDate____Canada: Due by xx/yy/zz £yyyyyyyDate____China Due by xx/yy/zz £yyyyyyyDate_____India: Due by xx/yy/zz £yyyyyyy

Choose your Countries and have a good think about which countries have the wherewithal and the ability to copy your product.Date_____Total minimum costs:-£yyyyyyy

Although the due date for the international phase is xx/yy/zz for non -European countries it is possible to pay penalties to get the patents in the months after the xx/yy/zz

The patent system is complex and difficult to comprehend, as it is so vast book (xxx) will cover the patent systems.

Appendix G

Chairman & Managing Directors Summary

(A 3-page pull-out of your Business Plan with a front cover making it no more than 4 pages in total)

Now I will show you how to produce your Chairman & Managing Directors Summary. This is a three page extremely condensed pull-out of your Business Plan and may be all you need to give to people who request to see a copy of your plan. In the armed forces this is called the 'General's & Admiral's'.

This document is the property of 'Your Business name.' and may not be copied or communicated to a third party or used for any purpose other than that for which it is supplied without the express written authority of 'Your Business name'

Put your logo here :-

NappyTime™
Changing Mat

snuggles™

'Your business name' ... and Products

Chairman & Managing Directors Summary

Business Address:

(Remember...You can use your accounts address as your Company official address and have your post sent to your working address)

Telephone: ....

Fax: .... **(By arrangement)**

E-mail:- ....

Websites ....

....

Gin's tips :- Worth considering having more than one website, more interesting, more prolific,

More than one window on your business world.

UK Patent Granted Number: ....

European Patent Granted : ....

Registered Design Number: ....

British Standards Test Report Number:

....

Document Number:- ....

Date Issued: ....

Updated: ....

Copy Number: 00x

Word File name : ....

The Project

The U.K. Product Template

The Birth rate in the U.K. is more than 1,000,000pa so we will always be working on a target market size of 4,000,000 potential customers, in any one year for the Standard NappyTime TM Changing Mat (0-36 months).

Your details here may be stating that there are x million 16- to 70-year-olds who drink let's say coffee as you plan to open a coffee shop.

1 Millions pregnancies + 1 Million (0-12months) + 1 Million (12-24mnths) + 1 Million (24-36mnths)

= 4 million potential consumers per annum

There will be potentially 1.5-3 standard mat(0-36mnths) units purchased for every child born in the UK. The target market rises to 6-12M potential customers due to sales to:- Baby Weighing Clinics/Child-Minders/Grandparents.

Another Example Template

[For instance: Your details here may be stating that there are x million 16 - 70-year-olds who drink let's say coffee as you plan to open a coffee shop.]

Priorities:-

Far Eastern or UK Manufacturer capacity up to 3 million mats per annum. Set up a Marketing System to publicise market and advertise the product for UK and Overseas customers.

Strategy

Through the disciplined application of a long-term business strategy, (Your business name) has the potential to double its revenues in the next decade and we are confident of reaching the majority of the 160 civilized Countries in the coming 10 years. The company has the potential to be a world-leading/County leading/ Village effective/Global leading provider of xyz products/ abc services for use by consumers, facilities, medical establishments, and children. The company operates in four long-term markets,

e.g., ...nursery, public facilities, medical, toys and books.

1. Addressing five global markets: E.g., ...Nursery Industry, Public Facilities Industry, Medical Industry, Toy Industry; Book Industry

2. Invest in design, technology, capability, and infrastructure

3. Developing a competitive portfolio of products and books

4. Focusing on growing market share and install product base

Vision

(Your Business name) has the potential to be a world leading/County leading/UK effective/Global leading/ village effective provider of xyz products for use by E.g., consumers, facilities, medical establishments, and children (Have a think which 4 main sets of purchasing person types will be your customers be?) and will establish a strong position in global markets – E.g., Nursery, Public Facilities, Medical, Toys and books.

It can already be envisioned that a major UK company will grow from the innovative products/services to be brought out over the next 10 years and into the future under E.g., the Patent already granted by the UK and European patent offices and on future patented products.

Product Sales Plan

Plan to sell to a minimum of 10% of E.g., birth-rate market-size by Year .... in the UK with inward growth funding from (Your Business Name) Further countries distributers/shops/offices/outlets/premises will be appointed.

Plan to sell a minimum of 25% of e.g., the birth rate in the top 70 countries in the world by the end of the Patent in Year........

Plan to sell main product and range of products to a minimum of 25% of the birth rate in the top 160 countries in the world by Year......... (perhaps ten years later)

The sales growth charts for each separate product/service/outlet/shop/premises will indicate sales potential given the ratios of the curve and the speed at which the sales line is ascending towards its plateau level this in turn will allow us to calculate the number of employees to recruit the workspace required etc...and the probability of sales values.

The sales predictions above cover the UK only/County only/across the World but e.g., ... as there are over 140 million babies born throughout the World every year the world target market is on a much wider scale. The granted patents cover the European Countries that have the capability of commercialising the products.

The Innovation

Significant technological advances within the product/service include:-

The use of a totally new xyz product/service

In addition, several patentable, innovative, and ergonomic advances for xyz types of persons are integrated into the one product m/service and are described as follows:-

New Design Features

List the novel/great design features of your product or service (In the case of a total new product that you have filed a patent for and are in your patent pending year ... anyone who views your business plan, or the product must sign your non-disclosure document until your product is published by the patent office)

In business is can be useful to get your business associates to sign non-disclosures anyway whilst your business is in its infancy.

(Your words here... regarding the status of your patents if they are involved)

All the above design features are patented under the one PCT/ UK and European patent.

Products to be launched over 20 years of Patents and Beyond:-

(Have a think about what you want to launch each year going forward over the next 20 years. Each launch takes time determination and planning .... Once listed here they will be your targets.. Achievable/not achievable it does not matter you won't know until you **LIVE it.**

(1)Year ....

(2)Year ....

(3)Year ....

(4)Year .....

(A) ......

(B) ......

(C) ......

(5)Year ....

(6)Year ....

(7)Year ....

(8)Year ....

(9)Year ....

(10)Year ....

(11) Year ....

(12) Year ......

(13) Year ......

E.g.,.....Accessories

(14) Year ....

(15) Year ....

(16) Year.........

(17) Year.........

(18) Year ....

(19) Year ....

(20) Year ....

The Four Industries

The current product for the Nursery Industry/ Medical Industry/The Public Facilities Industry and the Toy & book Industry includes one unit the xyz products

Put in here your own products/service

Define the various parts/versions of your product or service and the industry segments. Then go on to explain how you plan to go about selling, and explain which organisations you have approached to help you, and detail if you have enlisted your MP or any other Mentors/Business advisors who are supporting you. You can also indicate how these advisors are assisting you too. Then whoever is reading your plan will know that you have some expert guidance in your planning.

Product definitions:-

(i)

(ii)

(iii)

(Your Business) Activities Include:-

(1) Marketing and advertising the ....

(2) Formulate a 12-month rolling Advertising System.

(3) Aid overseas Distributors with Sales & Marketing material and Advertising Plans.

(4) Launch (Your business name) product .... in the UK and overseas.

(5) Provide Marketing Solutions in house and via PR & Marketing Agency(s).

(6) Plan to market and advertise all future products (once funding available).

(7) Prepare all the marketing material that surrounds the product i.e., including e.g., 4-Colour carton, V-card, Operating Instructions, Swing tag, 4-Colour Box, Merchandising Unit etc.

(8) Provide an information only/sales website.

(Your Business name) Additional **Business Activities Include:-**

(1) Preparation of Business Plan/ Marketing Plan/Market Research.

(2) Provide Manufacturer with drawings and Quality Plan and Product Specifications – Ensure products meet all Specifications.

(3) Form (Your Business Name) as a Limited Company/ Partnership/Sole Trader/Franchise

(4) Prepare all drawings and documentation to Manufacture the product

(5) Prepare Insurance of patent/Company/all shipments.

(6) Manufacture Sell and Deliver product to Retailers & Public Facilities.

(7) Gradually launch the full product/service range throughout the world over 20+ year period and beyond.

The Market

The (Your business product(s) name) is a branded Product and will be the platform for the small sized company as it sells itself and (Your business name) promotes it and with sales into e.g., Volume Retailers and Website Retailers and Public Facilities this provides a captive audience and can be replicated all around the world.

All the other products/shops/outlets will build the Company in the e.g., four Global Industries and support growth, which will have the protection of the patents and the copyright and the Trademark registration across Europe and the Branding across the world.

The market size of each product market throughout the world could run into vast financial rewards.

To end your Businesses Plan, include the following:-

('Your Company Name')

Company Number: yyyyyyyy

VAT Registration Number: yyyyyyyy

Registered address:

Consultants : List your consultants including your Accountant with their letters after their names.

Abbreviations

P.R = Public Relations

RRP = Recommended Retail Price

T.O. = Turnover

Ltd. = Limited Company

U.K. = United Kingdom

PCT = Patent Cooperation Treaty

OH = Over Heads

VAT = Value Added Tax

PA = Per annum

MP = Member of Parliament

UK = United Kingdom

SQ = Square Feet

LTD= Limited

PPHR = People per hour

Mn= Million

The Business Mountain – Don't look down
Test paper
Book 2 – Business planning

There isn't a one size fits all, but these questions will get you and students studying business thinking

1. What percentage of staff turnover per annum should flag up to you, there is a problem?

2. Explain what is a 'Financial Turnover'?

3. How many questions should be on a market research questionnaire?

4. What is blogging?

5. What will be the prices of your products in 10 other Countries according to their economies?

6. How many different types of marketing strategies are there?

7. How many babies are born in the whole of your Country each year?

8. What should you put at the end of your business plan?

9. How many websites does Virginia recommend you have for your business?

10. How do you go about describing the features of your product or offering?

11. How do you describe the benefits of your product or offering?

12. What is a SWOT analysis?

13. What is your SWOT analysis?

14. What is the purpose of a business plan?

15. In order to achieve success what 3 criteria must the business achieve?

16. Give 4 examples of typical capital equipment for your business?

17. What type of printing will be required for your business ie. leaflets posters ... etc?

18. What types of training are available for your type of business?

19. What type of premises will be suitable for your business idea?

20. What is the square meterage suitable for the business you are planning to startup?

I've had a few (close friends) draft readers, this is what they had to say:

"Give me the first seven chapters please" …. "Where are the next seven chapters pls? I need them". "I read her book really fast the first time, now I am re-reading it all over again much more slowly. (Launching an Antiques business with his wife).

JACK, CARE NURSING ASSISTANT

"Her book is my bedtime reading" with raised eyebrows and a big smile. (Wants to write a book on family in Africa's hereditary perspective on adolescents).

MAUREEN, RN NURSE FOR 30 YEARS

"Can I have the first seven chapters please?"…"OK, I need the next seven chapters now please, do you mind? … Jumped in the lift with me "Oh my God … Your book is amazing", "You are going to be known across the World for this" (Has already moved to Norfolk by the Sea to prepare for opening a B&B by the sea).

GOSIA, RN NURSE

"Oh my God Sis! Just started reading your book, it is amazing!!!! You've really made it simple, relatable, and easy to digest. Just started reading through it and I love it already. Wow!"

ESHER, FOUNDER OF ZEPHYREASE